Hedge-Rider

hedge-Rider

by Eric De Vries

PENDRAIG PUBLISHING, LOS ANGELES

Pendraig Publishing, Sunland, CA 91040
© Eric De Vries 2008. All rights reserved.
Published 2008.
Printed in the United States of America

ISBN 978-0-9796168-7-7

Contents

hedge-Rider: defining witchcraft

Often you here so called 'Wiccans' and 'Pagans' claim that they are 'Witches'. They fight for the environment, freedom of religion and other good things that will make this world a better place. However, when you ask them what Witchcraft is, what it stands for and what its most dearly held principles are, you get some vague story about 'the burning times' and words like 'responsibility' and 'nature religion' keep popping out. The word used most commonly is 'magic(k)', which isn't supernatural but, supposedly, 'proven' by science. To the new seeker they're a weird, fluffy New-Age bunch and don't seem to have any link to the ancient Witches. So, what is Witchcraft really about?

Searching for the roots of Witchery

For centuries, Witches have been regarded as wicked, evil women who try to harm Christian people by cursing their live stock, their crops or suck the blood out of their children. Normal human beings are, usually, not capable of doing such things and therefore people thought they had the ability to make magic. This ability was given to them by the Devil himself, who tried to torture innocent Christians as much as he could, and the Witches, the people believed, helped him. With the aid of politically and religiously motivated propaganda, this resulted in the hanging, burning, exiling and persecution of real and imagined Witches.

Though the above doesn't make the Witches look like really nice people, they often did serve a purpose in the community. Some were regarded as 'white Witches' or 'wise women' and helped the common people with herbal and magical remedies. Often functioning as midwives they were labelled 'Witch', especially when the mother or child had died while giving birth or soon after it.
However, Witches weren't always regarded as 'evil' which is demonstrated by the continental origins of the word – and the vast majority of the Witches. Modern Wiccans and Witches have talked endlessly about the English roots, without paying any attention to the continental ones. The Dutch word for Witch, 'heks', comes

from the Middle Dutch 'Haghetesse', which means 'Hedgerider' or 'spirit on the hedge'. The same goes for the root of the modern German 'hexe', which is Hagazussa, which also means Hedgerider, soul on the fence.

The term Hedgerider must have been almost universal in the Germanic languages. It appears in Old Norse as 'Hagzissa', but also in Old English as 'haegtesse' – shortened in the modern day as 'Hag'. The continental Germanic words for Witch clearly come from words meaning 'Hedgerider'. However, all this talking about 'Hedgeriders' doesn't answer our question immediately. The meaning is a bit vague: what's about riding a hedge? What does Hedgerider mean? And what does it have to do with Witchery?

The answer is found in the symbolism of the hedge. To our ancestors the hedge separated the village from the wild, outside world. Within the village you were protected by law and things were, more or less, civilized. At this side of the hedge everything was nice, humane and protected by Law and most important, it has *culture*. Outside everything was *wild*, dangerous and one could be attacked by animals and perhaps angered wood-spirits or other demons. Chaos was everywhere, waiting with its dark, sinister hands until you walk by. The hedge is the Boundary, separating the two and was thus an 'in-between' place. All this is symbolic of Middle-Earth and the Otherworld, as well as culture and the wild.

In the Swedish Law of Västgötaland it is said: "*Woman, I saw you riding on a fence with loose hair and belt, in the troll skin, at the time when day and night are equal.*" All this points to the Otherworldly nature of the Witch and the Hedgerider. The fence is the hedge, the boundary. The "troll skin" is, obviously, some kind of mask or guise in which the Witch dressed herself, as to be recognised by or invoke the Otherworldly powers. At the time when day and night are equal, the boundary is thought to be the thinnest. It isn't the Day, but not yet the Night, meaning it is the in-between time; the Otherworldly time.

11

The idea of the hedge is also found in the trial of Hans Buochman in 1572: "*he was carried away to a strange land; he did not recognize himself and was not in his right mind. He had gone through the forest by night and had happened on a gap in the fence, when he heard a rustling as if a mighty demon flew by, and immediately afterwards drumming, piping, and the sounds of strings.*" Apparently he went to the forest and when he passed through the fence he heard sounds of a feast, denoting his entrance into the Otherworld.

Middle-Earth or Midgart, this world, is symbolized by the village while the Otherworld is the outer world, the wild and dangerous forests. When you ride the hedge, one of your legs is hanging on the left while the other is on the right. You're in both worlds; you're on the boundary, being part of both worlds at once. Now things are starting to get clearer; the Hedgeriders weren't just people who enjoyed sitting on hedges all day, but who were able to travel between the worlds. They could be in Middle-Earth and the next moment in the chthonic spirit-realm. That is the true meaning of Hedge-Witchery: Witchery of the Otherworld.

The Otherworld has been and is known by various names such as Elphame, Elvelond, Wormsel, Faeryland, Niflheim, the Land of Faery, though most people will know it under the name 'Hell'. Although you might think of Hell as a fiery pit full of sinners, tortured by a satanic majesty; it is definitely not. Hell was the Germanic Underworld where the dead travelled and had another existence defined by both their virtues and sins. If you died gloriously in battle you went to Odin's Vallhöl, if you weren't chosen by Odin, then maybe Freya choose you go live with Her. If not, then you would go into the hall of Hell – though this isn't as black-white as it seems, some cults held that they would go live in the mountains, or stayed in their grave or burial mound. In Hell, you could live well, just as you spent the most of your life, or you could be 'punished' in the hall of the Goddess Hel. Niflhel was the lowest region, suited at the roots of the World-Tree, full of mystery, darkness, mist, the dead, where the really wicked were sent, preventing them from being reborn, keeping them from doing more harm.

The Hedgeriders travelled to this strange world and mediated its mystery back to midgart. With their ability to divine the future, to raise the dead, speak to the Gods and see into any of the worlds, they were as much feared as they were respected. The words 'Haghetesse' and 'Hagazussa' also refer to 'Hagedisse', which is a term applied to the priestesses of the Germanic peoples and they – the Hagedisse – fulfilled the same tasks as the Hedgeriders did.

As you might have expected, the Hedgeriders, and so the Witches, were everything but Christian. They still continued a Pagan practice and didn't think of the Underworld as a realm of punishment, but more as a place full of secrets to be uncovered and where wisdom was to be found. The Hedgeriders were the heirs of a long forgotten cult of priest(esse)s and travellers to the Underworld. With the passing of time, the ruthless persecution and the high death-rate in Medieval and Renaissance life, this cult was wiped out.

During the Witch-hunts, a lot of people were burned, hanged, exiled and of course, tortured. Often the hunters chased after their own, perverted fantasies rather than real Witches. Even though they probably murdered more Christians than real Witches, this does give us some testimonies about Witches. Of course we shouldn't over exaggerate the importance of these testimonies for they are obviously modified by the clergy or given under the pressure of torture. However, the essence is still there and can give us a lead in the search for Witchery.

In the testimonies there are certain elements which range from Christian imagination to real, often Germanic, Witch-beliefs. Although we have Witches confessing to have spit upon the crucifix and having sucked the blood out of babies, there are also Witches who have ridden through the sky with Frau Holle, Madame Oriente or Dame Abondia, or whatever name the Goddess was known by; and Witches who've journeyed across an immense river to the gate

13

of Hell and of course the appearance and worship of the, obviously Pagan, 'Devil'. The following passage is from Aelfric's Homilies, dating from 10th century England:

"Yet fares Witches to where roads meet, and to Heathen burials with their phantom craft and call to them the Devil, and he comes to them in the dead man's likeness, as if he from death arises, but she cannot cause that to happen, the dead to arise through her wizardry."

If you filter out the Christian elements, there remains important information about the Shamanic lore of the Hedgeriders. In this passage, it is clearly stated that Witches travel to the crossroads and Heathen burial mounds. Of old, crossroads have been considered entrances to the realm of the dead and places where the Dark Powers would gather. It is interesting to note that the gallows were erected at crossroads to confuse the angered spirits of the dead and so prevent them from haunting their executioners. Moreover, the gallows and the crossroads were sacred to the Germanic God Odin/ Wodan. Also, in Greek mythology, the crossroads are considered sacred to the Goddess Hecate, the Goddess of the Underworld, the dead and…Witchcraft.

Actually, the Heathen burial mound is a powerful entrance into the Underworld. It is the hollow hill where the Gods, the elves and the dead reside. From this mound the Hedgerider can summon the dead, a craft deeply associated with the Hagedisse, the Volva, Seidkona and Seidmadr of Norse Mythology and the Heathen God Odin.

More interesting and maybe even more Otherworldly, is the mentioning of "faring" and "phantom craft". This is actually a reference to the ability of the Witch to shape shift, which is skill deeply associated with the journey to the Underworld. For example, the werewolf is a "man-wolf" who is exiled from the village and is deemed to live in the wild forests: the Underworld. The Wolf itself is a symbol of Hellish Chaos and Dark Power and is deeply connected with the Gods of the Underworld. As a symbol of pure rage and dehumanization – and therefore 'Underworldization' – the ability to become a wolf, or any other animal, is the same as having the ability to travel to the Underworld. Moreover, "phantom" means Witchery is about the invisible spirits and the unseen itself.

This ability, the use of an animal shape to travel to "where roads meet", or any other place the shapeshifter chooses, was considered basic to Witchery. Actually male Witches were one called 'werewolves' in Holland. There are also numerous examples of shapeshifting from Norse Mythology such as the description of Seiðr, given in reference to the Shamanic God, Odin. Though Witches are said to travel in the shape of animals, they also travel upon the backs of animals. This practice is mentioned in the 10th century Canon Episcopi, one of the earliest and most influential Christian works on Witchcraft:

"During the night, with Diana, the Pagan Goddess, in the company of a crowd of other women, they [the Witches] *ride the backs of animals, traversing great distances during the silence of the deep night, obeying Diana's orders as their mistress and putting themselves at her service during certain specified nights."*

Instead of talking about shape shifting, this passage talks about the riding of animals. This practice is common throughout the Witch-trials and often the goat, hare or black dog is the vehicle of transportation to the Sabbath.

Also interesting is that the Canon Episcopi talks about 'Diana', the Roman Goddess. Although the Goddess appears in the Aradia, or the Gospel of the Witches, it's rather improbable that the Witch-Goddess actually is Diana. More likely, it was one of the Germanic Goddesses such as Holda, whose name appears in later editions of the Canon Episcopi instead of 'Diana'.

15

Though there has been suggested that the origins of the Witch Goddess is Celtic, I think this isn't realistic. The Witch-Goddess, Frau Holle for example, appears in Germany, which hasn't been influenced by the Celts. The Germanic peoples though have influenced – i.e. occupied – the southern countries, France and Italy and parts of Spain. Also, the places in which the Witch-Goddess Holda appears weren't occupied by the Roman armies, which wrecks the idea that Holda is a Germanized version of Diana.

When you connect the concepts described in Aelfric's Homilies and the Canon Episcopi, they lead up to quite an interesting concept concerning the Witches' Sabbath. Using their "phantom craft" the Witches travelled upon the backs of animals, or in the shape of animals, to the Meadow of the Underworld: the Sabbatical gathering. The place where the Sabbath was held was a fragmented corruption of the Underworld, as perceived by the Christian Witch hunters.

This intimate connection is further strengthened when taking a look at the lore of the Venusberg and the Underworld-Mountain. It is interesting that in parts of France, Germany, Italy, the alpine countries, there are mountains wherein a Goddess resides. Some of the German mountains are the Brocken, Schlern, the Hörselberg and many more. In Italy there appears Sibilia's Hill and the Cave of Madame Oriente. Anyway, the mountains were filled with elves who were reigned by one Mistress – Holda/ Venus/ Oriente/ Sibila/ Herodias – who resembles the Norse Goddess of the Underworld. She taught the Witches the Arts of Magic and Wortcunning. Remarkably, this hollow hill can be considered another manifestation of Hel's hall and provides us with more details about the Sabbatical gatherings of Witches.

Central within the testimonies and folklore is the journey to the Sabbath. The Witches would leave their bodies and travel to the Sabbath, or some other strange place, where they would meet the Devil or a Lady of the elves, 'Devils' and other Witches. When asked by the judges where this place was, they often described places that didn't exist. The Sabbatical gatherings probably took place in the realm of the spirits, the Gods and other mysterious beings. This is also suggested in the Canon Episcopi and the Homilies where the journeys are described as 'dreams'. This means the Witches travelled "in the spirit", a term often used to describe the lucid dreaming of the Witches. The Sabbatical gatherings took place in a different realm; the Otherworld. The journey to the Underworld was central within Witchcraft.

The Witches have left us a beautiful, spiritually complex heritage, which you will discover in this book, but they also leave us with some serious questions: "can one truly be a Hedgerider in the modern day? What does Hedge Witchery have to offer us? And, most important to the NeoPagans; can one be a Witch without being a Hedgerider?"

The Importance of Hedge Witchery for Modern Paganism

Different people will give different answers, however, from the above one can easily conclude that it's *impossible* to be a Witch without being a Hedgerider. Even though Modern Witches often say that Witchcraft was and is about nature magic, it is not. A lot of Witches who were tried for Witchcraft were practitioners of simple folk-magic, though to identify these people as Witches would be changing the essence of the word, Hedgerider. The core business of the Witches and their forebears was travelling to the Otherworld. Therefore it is impossible to be a Witch without travelling to the Otherworld – or at least have some sort of contact with it.

Hedge Witchery has a lot to offer us, one of its blessings being a form of native Shamanism. The necessity of this lies in the fact that today, all the forms of Shamanism practiced by Western people are stolen from other cultures – yes, stolen "taken without asking". Instead, Hedge Witchery has to offer a form of Shamanism that is native to our surroundings, embedded in our own unconsciousness and fits with our own archetypes.

Hedge Witchery, as much as every other true form of Paganism, offers a form of spirituality that breaks the boundaries placed upon us by modern materialistic and scientific thinking.

This thinking pattern completely rules out the spiritual, the divine and our personal soul. Hedge Witchery offers a way of believing and living which makes us part of the earth, which acknowledges our emotions and dedicates importance to them. Just like the other Pagan religions, it has never been at war with science and can, therefore, remain far from the superstitious beliefs held by the older religions, but also has the ability to stress the importance of science as a tool for a better world. Hedge Witchery gives meaning to life, to the entire ecosystem of the Earth itself. Along with the other Pagan religions, it offers a way of living far from the materialistic-scientific thinking which has lead to the problems of the 21st century; Hedge Witchery changes your view upon the world, and do I dare to say, into a healthier one.

Also, Hedge Witchery leads to a deeper understanding of culture itself and thus identity. As the ideas expressed in the book 'Dreamtime: Concerning the Boundaries Between Wilderness and Civilization', culture is better understood when the boundary between culture and wilderness is crossed. This is exactly what the Hedgeriders do. They cross the hedge, which is, among other things, the boundary between the Wild and the Civilized. A better perspective upon culture is gained through the temporary abandonment of culture; the journey to the Underworld. Practical results? The better appreciation and ethics of life.

In Search of Culture and Context

So, where are we going with all this? How can we re-discover Hedge Witchery and unravel its mysterious threads? There are two ways to go:

    i.) historical
    ii.) instinct and gut reaction.

I don't think one of them can produce a really healthy way of living, since history cannot tell us enough and instinct is probably not always true towards the historical. You might want to take a look at the new-age 'Witches' who just cannot separate facts from fiction, such as "Charmed" from reality.

In instinct, there is a possibility. What most of the Heathen traditions have is the strong connection with the Ancestors. They are the people who've gone before us, breathed the same air, looked almost exactly like us and of course shared our dreams and desires.

With the coming of generations, it is said, there are certain 'guides' passed on, inherited beings, spirits who are here to help. Sometimes they are 'just' spirits but mostly they are the spirits of long-gone relatives who remain with us through our blood and souls, the clan mothers of the old ways. Now don't think I'm a racist or fancy some other, disgusting, political philosophy, but the ancestry is, in a way, really important. The Ancestors may speak through our actions in ritual and spiritual moments, certain types of immediate "clearings" in mind or sudden insight into lore and life itself. These are given by the Ancestors, to help us recover our heritage.

My point is that it's impossible to rule out the feelings and personal insight. However, we should also trust the historical views upon mythology and accurate translation, etymology and the reliability of historical records. This book is a thin line between those two things and there will be a lot of claiming and interpreting around here. Though remember that books written based on history and trying to search for something spiritual, always, always will be opinionated and subjective.

I've had many debates about many things with both Wiccans and people who just refer to themselves as 'Witches'. The subject most furiously discussed, often leading to arguments and verbal fights and most important for a good understanding of Witchcraft, is the origins of Witchery and whether its roots lie with the Germanic peoples. So, before we'll be talking about Witchcraft again we'll have to find where it comes from.

The Witch-Cult itself must have been quite universal in the late Medieval and Renaissance period, since there are a lot of testimonies which seem quite reliable and also folklore and fairy tales appear in a similar manner throughout Northern and Central Europe. Witches appeared in the continental countries like Germany, Holland, Belgium, France, Italy, the Alpine and the Baltic countries, in Great Britain, there were also Witch-trials and in the U. S., though we cannot merely say those people were 'genuine'.

Many people have said to me that Witchcraft is 'universal' and that every culture has its "own Witches". Usually, they base themselves upon the definitions used by anthropologist who simply call everybody who practices (folk-)magic and isn't liked by everybody, a Witch. That's not true though. Even though I think humans are all capable of travelling to the Otherworld and that in many, many cultures there are people who do this; this doesn't make a Siberian Shaman or a practitioner of voodoo a 'Witch'. Actually they would be quite offended.

Culture and religion are tied up very closely and nobody – even though say they do – can truly be a cultural relativist. When confronted with brutal practices from other cultures, like we in the West consider the circumcision of young girls clitorises a barbaric practice, there will absolutely be no-one who will say "well yeah, that's only your view. It's a cultural thing and therefore it isn't wrong." People will always judge such things. Culture is important and in the old day your culture also defined your beliefs. That's why more ancient, isolated cultures just didn't have a word for 'religion', it was so tied up with everyday life that a distinction was impossible to make.

Witchcraft isn't a thing that just arose from Christian imagination, but rather something that was there before the Christians came and was then perverted by the Christians. Witches have survived to at least the early 17th century, however, the first records stem from the 9th and 10th century. That's a period of almost 700 years to bridge. Witchcraft must have been rooted deeply in at least something essential to survive that long. Symbols and archetypes are deeply embedded in culture and the archetypes of the Witch and the Witch-Gods are powerful archetypes as well, having remained for so long. Some credit goes to the Church for this; they actively kept the myths and symbols alive by their active persecution and repression. Anyway, people underestimate the energy that was spilled in search for and the destruction of the Witches. The Witch-cult, its myths and archetypes must have been powerful, or else they would not have lasted. Also, they should have been embedded in something essential which contained and sustained these archetypes, symbols and myths. Culture is the – only – reservoir for these things and thus, Witchcraft must have been deeply rooted in it.

Big parts of lore found on the continent carries Germanic elements. For example, what the Canon Episcopi talks about is also known as the Wild Hunt. The leader of the Wild Hunt is the Germanic God Wodan, though sometimes the Goddess Holda is said to be the leader. Anyway, the mythology carries definite Germanic elements.

Also, a lot of the things talked about when discussing and defining Witchcraft are also found in Norse Mythology, such as the ability to raise the dead through magic, the ability to shape shift, to see into the (other) worlds and to divine the future. Moreover, the countries in which Witchcraft is found – at least on the continent – are Germanic. Holland, Germany, the Alpine region, are all Germanic in tongue and roots. The etymology of the English word

21

for Witch comes from a Germanic language, just like the German and Dutch words.

Moreover, the areas in which Witchcraft is found were once under heavy influence of the Germanic peoples, Holland, England, Germany were Germanic and huge parts of Poland, almost touching the Baltic countries. The Alpine countries are/were inhabited by the Germanic peoples as was Italy, though only from the moment of the fall of the Roman Empire. France's original population was conquered by the Franks, Germanic tribes who strayed throughout Spain and Eastern Europe. The Celts were driven away, the Romans never came that far and surely the Greeks didn't.

However, there is another, good reason to 'choose' the Germanic People; they are our Ancestors. The English, the Dutch, the Germans – I wonder where that name comes from – are all Germanic. Even more, the Scandinavian peoples are Germanic and do I dare to say, great portions of the French and Italians, too. There is simply no other option. Stating that Witches are 'Celtic' doesn't stand up to the fact that the Celtic cultural influence had ceased to be in continental Europe by the times of the Witch-Hunts.

I'm not staying that other cultures are 'weak' or 'less' just because they are not 'Germanic'; that would be ridiculous. In fact, large portions of our culture aren't Germanic at all: only the roots of our language and large parts of the symbols and archetypes. However, nothing is more important than that: the symbols and archetypes through which the Underworld speaks. The Witch or Old Hag, the Toad, the Godmother, the Sorcerer, the (Were) Wolf, the Devil, the Ghost. In fact, a lot of these symbols are still alive and continue to exist in folk-traditions and fairytales surrounding children. For example, when I was a small kid, my mother would bake a cake on the 6th of January and hide a bean in it. The person who had the bean in his/her part of the cake was 'king'. This carries much of the symbolism of Noctifer-Lucifer polarity, Sacred King-cycle and the Twelve Days of Yule. Not to mention the entirely Heathen feast of

St. Nicholas, which is the Wild Hunt all over again.

That Witches were Germanic gives us access into the great reservoir of Germanic Mythology. Now, we can drink from the great well of Norse Mythology, of the Poetic Edda and all the other myths handed down, continental folk-tales, scriptures, fairy-tales – world-view, Cosmology and Gods and Spirits, all becomes clear: we have a context.

Hedge Witchery is not only a spirituality, it is also a religion and therefore in need of a mythos, a body of lore to put in practice, a set of symbols to speak in and to recognize the Gods by and to know the Otherworldly language by. Now that we've found that language – the mythology of the Germanic peoples – we can try to decode the messages left.

Otherworld Geography: The Metaphysics of Hell

The Underworld is key within our understanding of the Witching way, for we cannot fully grasp the reality of the Hedge-Rider's condition unless we understand both the worlds in which the Hedgerider lives. Although you might think: "I understand this world", this is definitely not the case, because this world, and your experience of it, is rooted *in* the Underworld. How? Read it yourself. But before we can talk metaphysics, we should see how the ancients thought of the Underworld and what they thought it looked like. First, we'll try a brief reconstruction of the Underworld according to Norse Mythology and then move into the delicate matters of the Witches' Underworld.

The Underworld in Norse Mythology

According to the Norse there are nine worlds, which came into being through quite a complicated process. Though I'm not going to get into all the details here, there are certain parts which remain essential. The worlds were sent forth from a vacuum, Ginnungagap, the Seething Void. At the two edges of this nothingness there were two 'worlds', Muspelheim and Niflheim. Niflheim was a world full of frost and mist, the name actually means, 'mist-world'. Niflheim was one of the two first opposites and can be equated to the side of frost and ice in the fire-ice polarity. Then, there is Muspelheim, which is the complete opposite of Niflheim: it is the world of fire. The two worlds are suited as opposites, Niflheim at the North with Muspelheim at the South. They are the two 'creative principles', the dynamic opposites from which the Seething Void was made. From their melting ice – 'water' – Ginnungagap, was created and from there the nine worlds were sent forth.

Interestingly enough, Niflheim *is* the Underworld, it lies beneath Midgard or Middle-Earth and is considered to be the realm of the dead. There's more to it though. Within Niflheim, it is believed, Hell is suited as an 'inner realm', which is specifically the realm of the dead. One could say that Niflheim is a 'greater realm' with

Hell lying in it[1]. Hell was the Underworld, where those that died of sickness or old age went, according to Snorri. However, in *Baldrs Draumar* it is clearly shown that this isn't the case as Baldr, who clearly hasn't died of sickness or old age, still goes to Hell. It may be that Hell wasn't a realm of punishment, reserved for those who didn't die an honourable death.

Some people went to Odin's Hall, Valhöll, in which eternal revelry and feasting is said to take place. A battle takes place every day, over and over again. Only at the Doom of the Gods will they go out to fight the Wolf. Only a few chosen men went to the Realm of the Gods, especially those who had worshipped Odin or died as a sacrifice to him.

The Hall of the Goddess, Hel, is said to be made of snakes stuck together and is a place where the dead reside. This Hall is sometimes also called Wyrm's Hall which means "snake's hall" and is still found in more modern lore under the name 'Wormsel' or 'Wyrmsele'. On the corpse shore, Náströnd, wicked people, oath-breakers, murderers and such were brought, and the snakes would drip venom upon them. Also a big serpent-dragon, called Nidhög[2], sucks the blood out of the wicked dead. On this beach,

1   In Gylfaginning, Brodeur Translation it is said about the Goddess Hel:
"Hel he [Odin] cast into Niflheim, and gave to her power over nine worlds, to apportion all abodes among those that were sent to her: that is, men dead of sickness or of old age"
She clearly lived within Niflheim, meaning that Hell might be a different world suited within Niflheim. Any-way, Niflheim must have been the encompassing world with Hell lying in it. In the Road to Hell, it is clearly stated that the author of the above quote probably tried to simplify Hell into a more dualistic concept: Hell = punishment, Asgard = reward while this isn't the case, obviously.
2   In Voluspa nidhög is identified as a serpent or maybe a serpent-like creature:
    "From below the dragon
    Dark comes forth,
    Nithhog flying
    From Nithafjoll;
    The bodies of men,
    On his wings he bears,

the corpses of evil men are torn apart by wolves, which might be an euphemism for the 'second death' by which their, clearly 'failed', souls are killed, torn apart by chaos – the wolf – to be recycled in the great cycles of nature:

She there saw wading
the sluggish streams
bloodthirsty men
and perjurers,
and him who the ear beguiles
of another's wife.
There Nidhögg sucks
the corpses of the dead;
the wolf tears men.
Understand ye yet, or what?

Voluspa, *Poetic Edda*

Between the dead and the gate to Wyrmsele there is a big river which is ice-cold and has knives flowing in it. There's only one bridge, which is made of pure gold, which crosses and connects the land of the living with the land of the dead. When the dead tread this bridge, they pass without a sound while the living fill the air with the noise of a thousand men. The guardian of the gate is the black dog, Garmr. He allows everybody, also the living, to enter but allows none to return. Interesting to note that in the Witch trials, the black dog is one of the infamous appearances of the Devil. All canine animals are deeply associated with the Underworld, the unseen and chaos itself. The dog functions as the guardian of the realm of the dead, much like the dog is the guardian of the human house.

The serpent bright:
But now I sink."

28

However, the wolf is the symbol the dark and bringer of chaos itself. Throughout the Saga's several wolves fulfil their task as chaotic, dark beasts. When the wolf, Fenris, escapes from his iron chains, the World-Tree will tremble and a 'Heathen Apocalypse' is upon us in which the nine worlds will be destroyed and the Gods killed. Moreover, the wolves or dogs are the beasts running with the Wild Hunt – another manifestation of dark, Underworld power. Ironically, some of the lore says the Wild Hunt hunts after one of the (wolf-) daughters of Fenris who tries to eat the sun – according to myth; this is why the Sun weakens when she closes in on Midwinter.

One account presents us with a nice picture of the Underworld. In the story of Hadingus, he sees a beautiful land where the herbs grow when it is Winter on Earth. Also, he sees an everlasting battle, much like the battle of Valhöll. There's a wall which separates this strange land from the rest of the Underworld and when the women who brought him there threw a dead cock over the wall, they could hear it crow from the other side, as if alive again.

There's never much said about the interior of the Underworld, what it looks like or what happens to the people who go there. The only possibility explained so far, is the resurrection of the dead in the Underworld dwelling, as suggested by the cock who's resurrected after being thrown over the strange wall. Hell seems to be two things at the same time: both a place of 'good' and a place of 'punishment', or rather retribution. The dreaded scenes of the corpse shore exist simultaneously with the fair land as described in Hadingus' journey to the Underworld. The passage into the realm of the Gods is an exception, reserved for those who were glorious and full of vigour. The majority of the dead souls had to go to the Underworld. In this place the really wicked and evil[3] were

3   *In modern new-age beliefs, people refrain from words like 'wicked', 'evil' or 'sinful', however, I think this only strengthens the meaning of these words. Anyway, I think one can clearly make the distinction between the word used for hideous and truly wicked acts of a serial killer and the use of the word 'evil' for every action or thought not conforming to the Christian doctrine.*

punished, ripped apart by the forces of chaos and then recycled through the process of nature. Also, few hints are given about a world even deeper than Hell in which the dead were kept who had done evil things. They died a 'second death' to keep them from being reborn again into the world of the living. However, the good 'live', or rather 'exist' quite nicely over there.

The Hollow Hills and the Witches' Underworld

Actually, in certain trials the geography of the Norse Underworld appears as almost identical to that of the Witch's journey. For example, in the trial of Thiess, a confessed werewolf, said that he and the other werewolves went down into Hell. To do that he had to cross a river, this river which separated this world and Hell is a common feature in the Norse depiction of the Underworld. Also the name used for the Underworld is the same in all Germanic tongues.

Certain Icelandic families believed that when they died, they were going to live inside a mountain nearby their house. In the Eyrbyggja Saga, a Heathen who held a specific mountain in great reverence thought that when he died he was going to live inside this mountain. After the Heathen was long dead and his family perished in a tragic accident, a shepherd saw the mountain being 'opened' and he heard sounds of feast and merriment: the Heathen's family had come to live with him inside the mountain.

The belief in a realm, kingdom or hall inside a hill as a place of the dead, is actually tied up very closely with Witchcraft, especially medieval, Witchcraft. The Witches were said to leave for certain sacred mountains in which their Mistress would teach them the art of wortcunning and magic. Travellers to the Venusberg reported that there was an ongoing feast of elves inside this hill. Not only the Knight Tannhauser travelled to this sacred mountain, also the Witches flew in their nocturnal journeys to the mountain of the Lady of the Elves where they were taught the ancient magical arts of sorcery and wortcunning. These elves weren't just nature-spirits or benign land-spirits, they were also the transformed souls of the dead – which is also why the elves lived in burial mounds. Once, a long time ago, they were the humans whose bodies were buried there. 'Elf' was the name by which some of the dead were known and sometimes the travellers reported that people they had known in life sat around the table and feasted with the Elf-Queen.

In Italy, the Lady of the Hollow Hill was called 'Wise Sibillia' and her Underworld Kingdom was entered through a grotto in the mountains of Norcia, a region famous for its Witches. More tales of the same kind appear all over this region.

In the mid 15th century, a Saxon astronomer wrote to a Italian friend asking questions about an Italian Mount Venus in which, supposedly, the magical arts were taught.

The Venusberg, which means 'Venus mountain', appears in Nider's Formicarius (1438) but also in Guerino il Meschino (1391). In Reductorium Morale (1360) and Libro de Varie Storie (1362), stories are told about a mountain with a realm inside full of – erotic – pleasures and, especially female elves. Moreover, the Goddesses associated with these Hollow Hills were also the female deities of the Witches and in several folk-tales and actual Witch-trials we are told that Witches travelled to the Otherworld Kingdom inside these sacred mountains.

They went to 'Game of Diana' or attended the gathering of 'Madame Oriente' inside the Hollow Hills. Inside the mountain, there is a gathering of elf folk, eternal feast, game and merriment but also they had to fight in "Her service" for the harvest. The elf hill is intimately connected with Witchcraft.

Often, Latin-educated clergy referred to the Lady of the Mountain as 'Diana' or 'Venus' while actually her name differs widely from region to region. In the Belgian and Dutch countries, she is known as Vrouw Vreke (St. Vreke) and as Vrouw Holle; in Germany she

31

is known as Frau Holle, Holda, Berchta or Percht; in the Alpine countries she is known as Berchta, Perchta, Holda or Holle and as Selene; in Italy she is known as Madame Oriente, Venus, Diana, or the wise Sibilla. She is the Goddess who is known by many names, with a kingdom in the hollow hill to which her followers, the Hedgeriders, journey.

Frau Holle or Dame Holda is said to live in the Venusberg, to which the Witches are said to travel. Also on the Brocken, Witches are said to gather. Scattered all over Northern Europe and the Alpine regions the Hollow Hills were the centre of the Witches' Underworld journey. They entered the Kingdom through the Venushölle, a cave leading deep into the heart of the Venusberg. Grottos, caves and lakes or wells near them were thought of as places of magical power and sometimes they functioned as entrances into the Underworld. Actually, certain physical places were thought of as entries into the Underworld. As said in the last chapter, Witches travelled to Heathen burial mounds where the Devil would appear in the shape of a dead man. Hedgeriders could enter the Underworld through these places; through the places which were thought of by the Christians as 'haunted'. These were the places more 'alive' and filled with the energy of the realm of the dead.

This is also why Witches congregated in old churches and graveyards, not because they were 'diabolical' but because these places had that feeling of death around them. To the ancients, death wasn't an evil happening, just something that happened and was inevitable. The Witches used the focus of 'death' and spirits in graveyards to ease the passage to the Underworld. Also, churches were often built on Heathen sacred sites to signify the superiority of the new religion over the old one. However, to the Witches these sites remained sacred.

In a fairytale, collected by the brothers Grimm, a young girl drops her spinning work in a well. Afraid of her archetypically wicked Stepmother, she jumps in the well to recover it. The girl loses her consciousness and wakes up in a beautiful realm underneath the Earth. Out of the goodness and industriousness of her hart she 'liberates' bread from an oven and apples from a tree. Eventually, she ends up at the house of Frau Holle. Frau Holle will provide her with food and give her a place to sleep if she is willing to work – she has to shake Holle's sheets so that it will snow on the earth. Although Frau Holle takes care of her, the girl eventually gets homesick and wants to return home. When she walks through the gate to Mid-World, she is covered in gold. When her lazy Stepsister dives into the well, she refuses to work – she burns the bread, doesn't relieve the apple-tree from its burden, nor does she shake the sheets of Frau Holle. When she returns through the gate to Mid-World again, she is covered in tar.

In this story Frau Holle appears as the strict, though just, mother who, again, is the Lady of an Otherworldly realm, suited beneath a well. In the next chapter we'll positively identify Frau Holle with the Underworld Goddess Hel. Again we see a happy Underworld with a more negative connotation of retaliation. Frau Holle is the Mistress of the Underworld, a world full of happy scenes, but also the horror of the corpse shore, both merriment and eternal feasting and the punishment of the oath-breakers and truly wicked souls. The sacred mountain, Holle's Hill, is the realm where the Witches travelled: the Underworld of the Hedgerider, the forest of wolves, suited beyond the boundary of Middle-Earth and the human mind.

Wisdom and the Underworld

Although we now know that Witches travelled to the Underworld Kingdoms of Wyrmsele, Hell, Elphame, Elvelond, we still do not know *why*. That's the key question: *why?* Why should you risk a journey to a place from which you might not return; a road hidden and covered with all sorts of tests and perils?

33

A wise giant tells us the secret:

"Of the runes of the giants and all the Gods,
I can tell with truth.
I have been to into nine worlds below, to Niflheim;
There men die out of Hel."

Vafthrudhismal 43

Basically, this means he has become wise through his journey to Niflheim, which gives us an important clue: the purpose of seeking contact with the Underworld is the search for wisdom. Of course, there are other reasons such as the search for knowledge which, obviously, can be found amongst the dead. Actually, this is a more necromantic variation upon the journey to the Underworld. The journeys seem to be centred around two things: either some dealing with the dead/knowledge/the thirst for magical power or the quest for wisdom. However, the first should be seen as a side product of the second.

The Well of Wisdom is situated inside the Underworld, which was guarded by the Giant Mimir and is also called Mimir's Well or Mímisbrunnr. Odin/Wodan, the Great Allfather of the Germanic pantheon, went to the Underworld to drink from Mimir's Well and so become all-wise; he was after wisdom.

Hidden in a place where no one wants, nor dares to go, wisdom is a treasure acquired in a dangerously deadly world. Wisdom, the key to the full blossoming of our gifts, is suited in a world full of death and the road to it is covered with all sorts of perils and test. It's a big treasure though. Basically, the Underworld is a place of wisdom and of death, darkness and chaos. Wisdom can only be found here, not in the nice heavens or on Middle-Earth: only between the dead does wisdom reside and only there can it be found.

If one goes to the Underworld and drinks from the well of wisdom,

Mimirs Well, one becomes 'wise'. That sounds nice and mysterious, "wise" but what does "wise" mean? What is wisdom?

First, we should define the exact meaning of wisdom. Most people will define it as "doing the smart thing", but that's a bit too difficult as "the smart thing" can be and almost always is subjective. Actually, the mystery is already in that sentence, "the smart thing", how can one know the "smart thing" if it is subjective, mean different things to different people? The point is that the "smart thing" is THE thing, the true thing. A wise person can twist the definition of 'smart', breaking the boundaries which culture and the human etiquette has placed upon us – in this sense the Hedgeriders were the wise people, as they were the only ones able to break through the boundary of culture and roam the wild forests. The "smart thing" is the only, truly good option, as it is not confined by human standards and is not subject to the strange idea of "subjectivity". The wise people know truth when they see it and when it comes to their actions they have an objectivity which surpasses culture, opinions, human standards and etiquette: they know truth when they see it and can act upon it – they can do the smart thing because they now the smart thing.

If "to be wise" is to know the truth and act upon it, then what is wisdom? When to be wise, means 'wise', then wisdom must mean the long term goal. "Having wisdom" is the objective and "having wisdom" might just mean that you "have truth". As we've seen from the last reasoning, you are "wise" when you "know truth". Therefore, is it right to say that to have wisdom is to have truth? I think so, the only distinction between wisdom and truth is that the *experience of truth* is what humans call wisdom.

Wisdom means the "experience of truth" then there should be something like truth, right? Truth is the 'essence' from which everything is derived, and the state of complete and ultimate objectivity. Truth is the "stuff" of the Gods, it's the thing. Truth is the face of the Gods, is the face of Hell and Heaven, of providence if you like.

The conception of truth is key when you want to understand the metaphysics of Witchery. However, the problem about truth is that it can't be communicated, not like symbols can be explained or commented upon. Truth is the Source, it's the Unknown, but at the same time it's everywhere. There are metaphors to describe truth, lots of them, but none can explain truth to someone who hasn't already experienced it.

Truth is a medium, the common reality that binds all together. Although truth sounds like it has an opposite, such a thing cannot exist. The only thing that is opposite to truth is illusion, and as the word itself already explains; it's an illusion, something not real. Or the opposite could be subjectivity. However, subjectivity is something only apparent in the human/animal consciousness, which has to do with the way we experience things, but certainly is not how they really are. With direct knowledge of truth, subjectivity is erased. When objectivity has been reached, subjectivity appears to be an illusion: it's a matter of gradation, not of opposites.

Everything takes part in truth, only not everything and everybody is conscious of it. This is second within this philosophy; not everybody is conscious of truth and therefore, not conscious of the all-connectedness of the Universe. People have the tendency to think of themselves as separate, because they *perceive* themselves as separate. Nothing could be farther from the truth. This is one of the 'illusions' of which Traditional Witches speak, and is one of the 'tricks' of the subjective mind to ensure our survival when we were still animals. But when truth is conceived and wisdom blossoms, a true state of objectivity is reached, then the boundaries of the mind are broken and can one fly over the hedge.

Truth is the medium of connectedness, connecting everything, it is the root of all – the inner reality, the root of existence. Truth lies at the heart of the worlds and is the origin and ending. From truth, everything is sent forth and everything shall return to it when the time comes. The inner reality of the worlds, the root of the cosmos *is* the Underworld. In Norse Mythology, this is shown through the order in which the worlds where created: first the Underworld, Midgard and then the Heavens. Also, the roots of the World-Tree which upholds all the Worlds, spring from a place somewhere deep inside Niflheim.

The inner reality of life is Hell, in Niflheim in the inner -world, the Netherworld, the Underworld: this is the inner reality. Truth resides in, *is the Underworld,* and when you drink from the Well of Wisdom, inside Niflheim, then you take part in the unseen and taste the waters of wisdom, experience it, you become it – you've found and experienced truth.

A Brief Introduction to the Conception of the Soul

Truth isn't actually a 'thing' in the sense that it is a piece of material, but rather a condition meaning that one can be a chair, for example, and find itself being true. Truth, or rather, the "thing" we're talking about can be equated to Godhead. Now, Godhead is NOT something like God; it's not a being, nor has a will of its own. Godhead is something very different. Godhead is the truth that lies at the heart of things and is that which makes everything one. Godhead is in everything and is the 'stuff' of truth.

Now, this isn't Christian or monotheistic it is pantheistic: Godhead or 'God' is in everything. As the essence of every human being and of literally every-thing, Godhead can be seen as the soul, the self, the essence of the physical experience. After all, the occult maxim appears to be true: "Thou art God", for Godhead is within you.

Even though everybody thinks of his personality when it comes to the soul, this isn't the ancient conception of it. The soul is impersonal – it has to be, since my soul is a "little piece" of Godhead – and therefore cannot contain memories, personality, dreams etc.. Soul is truth; my soul is, in essence, your soul and also the soul of the world. Another word for soul is self, meaning that our true nature is rooted inside the soul: my-self.

This means there's a real distinction between the physical and the inner parts of ourselves. Our consciousness is created by the cooperation of the body with the self. However, if the self would cease to exist, the mind couldn't exist much longer. The flow of life-force between the unseen and the body would cease to exist – this basically means death.

Though the self and the physical are definitely different in the sense of their properties, they certainly do NOT exist in a different place or plane. My soul is also inside my body. However, the soul is able to separate from the body, but the body isn't able to do this. This is the mystery of the Underworld-experience: the soul can travel to the Underworld, leaving the body as if asleep; but the body can't move without the soul.

Also, the true meaning of wise, "to experience truth" gets a totally new meaning when applied to the conception of the soul. The experience of truth is *exactly the same* as the experience of the self, as the self and truth are one and the same thing. Doing the "smart thing" is intimately tied up with the occult maxim: "know thyself", or rather "know thy self". This is the essence of the quest for wisdom, knowing thy self. This is also why Witches travel to the Underworld and why wisdom can be found there, because this is the reality of the self.

Though the words 'inner reality' and 'Underworld' sound different and separate from this world, they are not. Everything is connected and everything is at 'one' place, there's only One World. The only thing that makes us believe that they are separate is that we *perceive* them as "separate". Physical and non-physical, inner and outer, are just expressions of the same basic truth, Godhead.

38

When walking around on this planet, we see only the physical things. When walking around in the Underworld, we only "see" the inner, unseen things. Though, in reality they are connected and one and the same. This world, Middle Earth, is the Underworld and the Heavens at the same time. From the One Thing, from Godhead, they're both expressions and the only thing standing between direct contact with the unseen World, is the illusion that they are separate.

At fate's Well: The Wyrd Sisters and frau holle

Between the roots of the World-Tree there is a well, sacred to the Goddesses of Fate who sprinkles water from the well upon the tree, so it may grow high and tall. Their names 'are 'Future', 'To Become' and 'Shall'. They are said to weave the Fate of men and most importantly the Wyrd of the worlds. Weaving and twining the threads of Fate, they have the power over life and death, happiness and sickness, success and misery, prosperity and poverty.

Wyrd and the Basic Conception of Fate

To the Germanic peoples, Fate or rather Wyrd was an important concept. Most people think of 'Fate' as something that determines the course of your life, much like the idea of destiny, in the sense that someone has to do certain things in a certain way and cannot do differently. You *have to* move that way, touch those places, take those steps, even when their choice would have been the other way– they can't help it. This is the common idea of Fate.

Wyrd is quite the opposite. According to Wyrd, our future is determined by the past. Previous education, culture, experiences etc. have shaped you and made you the way you are; you are your past. "You" are your body, your genetic make-up and the experiences from the past. In the present, the forever and forward-going experience of now, you make your choices, as the 'past-you'. Therefore, everything you do will turn out in line with the past.

Your Fate is completely determined by the past. Basically you will never make a choice that isn't 'you'. You will always decide the way you decide, nothing can change that. On the foundation of the things you've seen and experienced before, you'll make your decisions, because these things have shaped your personality – your personality decides and thus makes a choice which can only be 'yours', even if you don't like the choice you have to make.

Basically, the concept of Wyrd is based upon the idea that everything happens for a reason. Reason doesn't mean it has a 'meaning', but rather every action, every movement is caused by another movement which has been caused by another movement. The movements of today are a reaction or consequence of the past. Following this, everything is caused by the past and so the things you face today, in the present, are a product of the past. Here you have the reason for the names of the Weird Sisters, all relating to the future: Fate is a continuous process of becoming, not predestination.

From the inevitability of making a decision that can only be 'you', everything will have to turn out a certain way, eliminating the endless possibilities and choosing only one, which has always been the only possibility since Mother Nature conceived you. Everything is caused by something else. Everything happens because of an action taken or not taken in the past, and all is set in motion after the first drop melted from Niflheim. Since then, everything will turn out only one way and this is the only way things can be: all is as it should be.

This might sound strange, as things seem rather mad at this time, the hunger in some parts of the world, the gangs in Port au Prince and New York, Bush in office, Sunnites killing Shiites, the multicultural problems in Western countries with Muslim minorities, and then there's the common genocide, racism, murder, rape etc. Everything could be much better right?

The point is, everything *couldn't* have been any different as we're all the consequence of an action taken before. Mind my words though, I'm not saying anything like 'the bad comes to the bad'. All I'm trying to point out is that everything that happens today has a *reason*, however this doesn't mean it is a *reason with a meaning!* Fate isn't moral.

Most people have the idea that they have the possibility to choose and have a free will. Ironically enough, these people only have the illusion that they can choose; in fact their future is already existing in their past.

43

Western civilization has a very strange obsession with free will; everybody should be able to choose. Though that seems a good basis for law and politics, one might wonder how realistic it is. We're more influenced by our surroundings than we might realize. Wyrd leaves some room for free will in the sense that you still have the illusion that you're able to choose. However, you still have to make the choices – even though your Wyrd already is, from the moment you were born everything was already there. In essence, everything will unfold in only one way, although the way it will unfold is NOT written in stone: Wyrd will unfold in only one way, which is exactly how it should be, and the only way it could be, but it is changeable in the now.

However, all this doesn't mean you have no possibility to change your Fate. Time exists in two states, present and future/past, which are essentially the same. If you can change the present, the past will change. In an instant, the present will change into the past and therefore, change the future and your Fate. To change the present is anything but easy. In an instant you have to let your past, your previous experiences, education, culture, go – just let it go. Then you can make the decision and take a route not yet explored, a path never taken. This is done by the immediate rethinking of every decision you have to make. Just let go of your "programming" and take a decision which you normally wouldn't make: do the smart thing.

The concepts of soul, Godhead and Fate are intimately tied up and without one, the other could not exist. According to Wyrd, everything, everyone is a 'strand', a 'thread' from which new things arise, new manifestations come to be. But where do these 'manifestations' come from, where does the process begin? It cannot begin in 'nothing' with the thread ending when someone dies, for the ancients believed that humans lived on after their deaths. Here, the concept of the soul comes in. At the heart of each strand lies the immortal quality we call the soul, truth or Godhead. From that soul, new manifestations come forth and therefore are subject to the condition of Wyrd.

The concept of Fate states that everything is a strand or a thread, woven into the tapestry of the Universe. At the heart of every strand, there lies the true Wyrd, the Well and also the soul from which the physical and the non-physical emerge. So, from truth comes the physical where everything seems to change, but in reality it doesn't – truth is still there only the shape it takes changes.

Wyrd basically says that from the past, the future immediately emerges and that changing your past is therefore, changing your future: the past and the future are one and influence each other. So the physical changes, but only in accordance with truth or 'different' souls changing each other's manifestation, or the opposites; Fire and Ice changing each other, transforming each other and hereby creating truth and oneness.

Half Black & Half White: the Goddess of Fate

Fate, Wyrd, weaves your life and your death, your career, your sins, your happiness and your misery. As you've probably noticed, Fate can be cruel, taking life when still young, massacres, genocide, rape, murder – all are Fate's creations. Life is not necessarily nice and most people suffer: this is their Wyrd. Fate destroys life, destroys happiness and takes everything you always wanted. However, Fate also gives life, gives happiness and gives the things you've always wanted. Fate is both cruel and caring. She's both mother and murderer.

This is an important feature of Wyrd. Although it is a process which is amoral and cannot 'judge' whether something is 'good' or 'bad', it definitely has a positive (creation) and a negative (destructive) side. This is shown in the tale of Frau Holle in which one of the girls is given gold and the other one is given nothing but tar. This signifies both the positive and negative side of Fate. Moreover, this is also shown in human life itself: a child is born and grows and grows with Fate often taking a 'caring' role towards children, while later on in life destroying their bodies and eventually killing them. The Ladies of Fate have usually been depicted as Three Sisters, Shakespeare's Weird Sisters, standing besides the cauldron. They appear as a sign of impending kingdom, to predict the Knight's future. However, sometimes their message isn't happy or glorious, sometimes it is death, punishment and terror.

In folk-tales and songs, murderers are sometimes visited by their dead victims who inform them about their unlucky Fate. The dead, the Otherworldly beings, the elves are often messengers of Fate, predicting coming sickness, war or death and sometimes prosperity.

Elves are deeply tied up with the Underworld. In folklore, the Lady of the Hollow Hills is also called the Lady of the Elves and presides over a inner kingdom crowded by elves. Sometimes people thought of them as the long-gone dead, or sometimes God-like nature spirits and sometimes they are the Genius Loci, the spirits of a place who have merged with the land. In some branches of traditional Witchcraft, it is believed that when death takes over, one ceases to be human and transforms into an elf, though only to reincarnate as human. Either way, they appeared as beings intimately connected with the Underworld.

Though the elves and the dead often appear as messengers, there is one supreme Goddess of Fate. She is the ultimate messenger. The Lady who stands behind Fate's double face is the Lady of the Witches. She's half dark, half white; which signifies her creation and destruction aspects.

To the Shepherd of Luckenwalde the Lady of the Elves, Frau Holle, appeared fair from the front, but hollow and rotten from the back. Frau Holle who lives inside the Venusberg is said to have the same appearance. Sometimes Frau Holle appears as a woman with a half black and half white face. Her appearance is intimately tied up with the cruel and compassionate workings of Fate.

In folklore, Frau Holle is intimately connected with spinning and therefore, Fate. Once, Fate was intimately associated with spinning and actually equated to it. From Norway to Italy and from Russia to Ireland, the image and lore of the Old Goddess was once well-known. Although the different, cultural-specific names differ and certain aspects appear definitely different, Her association with spinning is very clear.

In the twelve nights after midwinter, Frau Holle was said to reign Midgard. During this time, according to several folk-traditions, one should have finished spinning or else Perchta, a local name for Frau Holle, would wipe her ass with the flax still left. Also, spinners should not continue spinning during the twelve nights, because Frau Holle, who is the Goddess of Spinning, would curse them and send them bad luck while rewarding the hard-working who stopped during the twelve nights – actually paying homage to Her, saying that She was the ultimate spinner, recognising her power.
During the Mother's Nights, another name for the Twelve Nights, the natural order is reversed and Misrule rules. Traditionally, Wodan – whom we'll get back to in the next chapter – led the Wild Hunt during these nights, but early accounts assure us that also Frau Holle led the Wild Hunt.

Actually, the Twelve Nights are the most potent times for operations of Witchcraft. It is said that during the twelve days after midwinter, the Wild Hunt and other Otherworldly powers roam freely across Middle-Earth. In these twelve days – have you ever counted the days between the arrival of the three wise men at Jesus' birthplace and Christmas? – the world order is reversed, the boundary is thinner.

In Phulsborn, a man went at night to a mountain where he meets "Frau Hulle" spinning industriously. A big pile of flax was in front of Her already finished, with a small amount still to her right. She asked the man to take the flax, but he refused saying that he already had enough at home. Still, some of the flax ends up in his shoe and when he walks away his foot hurts, the flax had turned into gold.

A similar thing happened to the children in Kyffhauser. They too saw 'Frau Hulle', spinning industriously and she gives them flax. All the children throw the flax away, except for one girl. When they reach their home, the little girl's pockets are full of gold.

In Weingarten, a bridge stands before an old ruined castle. At night an old woman would spin and the people would hear the sounds of the spinning wheel. Also, in Germany people worshipped a Wood-Woman, especially during the twelve nights, also known as the *Zwölften*. They would spin the flax and sacrifice it to the Wood-Woman by burning it in the fire.

Moreover, on the castle hill near Biesenthal, a white lady appears with a golden spinning wheel in her hands. In Neu-Berstein near Gernsbach, a woman came to help the girls who had to spin too much for the lord of the castle.

Frau Holle is the Goddess of Spinning, as well of the home and industriousness and you can clearly see how these two are mingled in the above tales. Frau Holle helps you, gives you gold or something else if you are willing to stick with her.

Sometimes even the mother of Jesus adopted Holle's spinning aspect. In the medieval song the Mariënfaden there is said:

"Maria, good she could spin,
That womens' thread"

In Mecklenburg, it is said that when the flax isn't spun by the time the Zwölften begins, Frau Wod or Frau Gaue will come. In the Preignitz Frau Gode will come; in Untermark 'Frick' will appear; in the Harz the original name sometimes appears, Frau Frien or

Frau Freke. All these names are worn-down names or titles of the name Frick or Freya or one of the feminine versions of the name Wodan. We might want to notice that in a folk-tale surrounding the Venusberg, it is said that within this mountain the storm-spirit Wode resides together with his wife Holda.

Ultimately this leads again to the idea so over-appreciated within modern Wicca of a female divinity and a male divinity as the Gods of the Witches. However, as we shall see, Frau Holle is chthonic, dark and very different from the all-sweet female of new-age Paganism, who can hardly be considered a woman.

Frau Holle is the Goddess of Spinning, as clearly shown through the above discussed folktales and folklore. However, this means that She is the Half White Half Black Goddess of Fate. She is the one who determines the course of our lives, who gives us happiness or misery, kills us or gives us another life. From Her womb we were all send forth and to Her we shall return to Our Lady of Fate.

Half Black & Half White: Goddess of the Underworld

The Goddess Hel, according to the Proza Edda, has a face which is "half blue-black and half flesh-colour", this resembles the image of the Underworld Goddess, Frau Holle. Both appear as Goddesses of the Underworld and can be linked through their appearance and etymology of their names.

The Proto-Indo European Goddess Kolyo, means 'the thing gathered to cover'. This refers to the covering of the dead with earth, especially in burial mounds and grave hills. From the root 'kol', meaning hollow, the words hill, hall, hole, hollow, Hell and the name Hel are derived. All this meaning, or having some connotation of being 'covered' – i.e. buried. Also the name Holda/ Holle is derived from the root 'kol', basically stating that Holda/ Holle *means exactly the same* as Hel, as they are derived from the same source. They are essentially the same Goddess, both Queens of the Underworld.

Actually, the association of Frau Holle with the Underworld runs quite deeply through medieval accounts of Witchcraft and the sacred mountains. She was said to live in mountains, often accessed through caves and grottos.

In the mid-1500's tales are told about the Cavern of Sibillia, an Elf-Lady who lives inside the hill. Every night she and her followers turned into serpents. The association of the Queen of the Underworld or at least her Otherworldly kingdom with serpents is profoundly strong. As you might remember from Chapter Two, Hell was also called Wyrmsele, the Hall of Snakes and in several folktales the Hollow Hill is inhabited by elves who turn into serpents every Sunday or Saturday.

The strong connection between certain mountains, the Witch-Goddess and the Underworld might explain the strong association between the mountain called the 'Brocken' and Witches. The Brocken lies in the Harz-region, and at Walpurgisnight or May Eve, the Witches flew en masse to the Brocken, according to the earliest information, to fight with evil demons. Ironically, more recent information tells us that they were just kissing the Devil's bottom. Anyway, mountains were often regarded as sacred to Frau Holle and more generally to the Witch Goddes. That's why the Hedgerider went there; because there the boundary was thinner and the Cavern of the Goddess was there, the entrance to the realm of the Lady of the Hollow Hills.

Wells are associated with Frau Holle and often function as entrances to Her Otherworld realm. In Tegernfelden, in a mountain a White Lady reigns over several beautiful halls. Against the wall, the souls of old men are positioned. In a second hall, the souls of young men and girls sleep. In a third, a huge number of small children are lying down as if asleep. At the centre of every hall there is a well in which the souls destined to be reborn are purified.

In Hessen, Germany, a magical well or lake gives children to the women who take a 'bath in this body of water. This well is also known as Holda's Lake and the bath taken by the women is called a 'Hollenbad'. Under the well, there lies a realm in which the souls of the unborn children reside, waiting to be reborn. In this tale you can clearly see the Underworld realm of Frau Holle as the womb of the Earth Goddess – whom we'll get back to – but more importantly She is, again, associated with an Underworld realm.
This tale shows the association with the magical well through which entrance is gained into the world of Frau Holle. As you might remember from the last chapter, in the fairytale of Dame Holda, a young girl gained access into her Otherworld by jumping into a well.

The association between Holle's Underworld and the child-giving well runs quite deeply. The concept is always the same: a woman takes a bath in a lake which is said to be the entrance into Her realm in which children are waiting to be born. We'll deal with this more extensively later.

Frau Holle is also often called Mistress of the Hill and throughout Germany and Holland, so called 'Hollebergen' are spread. One of these is the Hörselberg, which is often equated to the Venusberg in which Holle is said to live. Suited between Hilgerhausen and Kammerbach the 'Hollestein', which means 'holle's rock', hides a cave which leads into the kingdom of Frau Holle. In Holland, in the national park 'de Veluwe' there's another Holleberg.

Frau Holle as the Mistress of the Underworld is most clearly shown in the trial of Diel Breull, a male Witch in Hesse, Germany. He said that he travelled to the Venusberg in which "Frau Holt" showed him the sufferings of the dead reflected in a bowl of water. Frau Holle is the Queen of the Underworld, showing her half black and

51

half white face as Mistress of the Eternal Feast and as Mistress of the Corpse Shore. She is the Goddess of the Gallows, dragging the dead by a noose around their necks into the Underworld, claiming them completely.

Half Back & Half White: Goddess of the Earth

Though Frau Holle might have been a Goddess of Fate and the dead, she is more than just that. She is also the Goddess of Fertility, Spring, the Earth, Children and the Seasons. She is also the Goddess of sexual fertility to whom people prayed for prosperity and a good harvest. They left offerings out on the roof or a seat on their tables for Her so that she would be grateful and bless them.

But what does "Goddess of the Earth" mean? For we certainly have no folktales about Frau Holle referring to Her as "Lady of the Earth". The title "Goddess of the Earth" is used to describe the aspect of the womb, as a life-giving and prosperity bringing element. Basically, this comes down to the idea of Frau Holle as a Goddess of a) fertility, children, prosperity, sex, marriage etc.. and b) motherhood, meaning She is the Mother who birthed everything into existence.

Frau Holle is commonly associated with children and childbirth. As discussed before, certain wells considered sacred to Her were said to increase fertility of the women who bathed in them. Also, children were thought to come out of wells. In Flensburg, there's an old, stone well from which the children are pulled. In Bettenbrund, near Bergheim in Bovenhessen, there lies the children-giving well called the Schwarzenbron. In the well of the Balkäuser Valley, children are said to come, sent by the Holy Virgin who assumed many of the aspects and rituals once attributed to Frau Holle.

At the slope of the Einzelberg, lies the Hollerwiese. Once a woman saw a bag full of gold, and put her new born down to take the gold. When she looked again, her child was gone. Crying she went home. The Priest advised her to return a year after the mysterious disappearance of her child. When she returned a year later, her child was sitting there, well fed and laughing. The child told her that a woman who lived inside the hill – the Einzelberg – brought him milk and fruits everyday.

Again, we see the caring aspect of Frau Holle as the protector of children. Also, Holle is the Mistress of the Wild Hunt. Unbaptized children were said to roam with this Hunt, specifically when led by Holle. This might be rooted in the Heathen idea that an unnamed child had no ancestral spirits or fylgia and so weren't protected. By joining Frau Holle, She took care of them and guarded them, instead of the ancestral powers.

Not only does She bring fertility in sense of children, she also is the Matron of Marriage and governs the more sensual aspects also attributed to Freya. In fact, Freya and Holda are in several ways one and the same. As said in the part about the Queen of the Underworld, Holle is the same as Hell and, according to Alby Stone, can be considered almost the same as the Nornir. Moreover, the Norse Goddesses Freya and Hel have a lot in common. Freya is *also* a Goddess of the dead – She is entitled to half of the slain according to Norse Mythology – and She even presides over Her own realm of the dead, Folkvrangar. Freya is the Goddess of the Dead, and love, marriage and fertility, the same goes for Frau Holle as She is intimately connected with Freya. The name Holle appears in medieval folktales in one breath with the name Freke, Vreke, which are – bastardised – continental names for Freya.

Just as spinning, the marriage was considered sacred to Frau Holle and in Her Twelve Days around Christmas, she prohibited any activity sacred to Her on the punishment of Her curse – which was quite a punishment as She was the Goddess of prosperity. Therefore no marriages were blessed in the Zwölften because Holle would curse them – actually this practise is still continued; between Christmas and Epiphany, none marry.

Holle had many, often local, manifestations. Among these are the Goddesses Perchta and Berchta, who mostly appear in the Alpine region. These Goddesses functioned the same way as Holle, as matrons of fertility and prosperity. Instead of the people sticking to the sober and sterile image of the Virgin, they preferred the appealing and sensual image of the Mother. The Mother was everything but dead, as shown by the complaints of a 13th century Priest who said that the young people preferred to pray to Perchta instead of offering prayers to the Holy Virgin. In later centuries Holy Marie adopted elements of Holle, such as Her patronage of marriage and the devotion of women in want of children.

Lying at the root of the mysterious "White Lady", Holle appears as a beautiful young lady cloaked in white linens. With Her long, blond and curly hair She enchants every man passing. She is invoked by the common folk as Mistress of the Woods and Animals, bringing fertility to the fields and to humans. Her totem is the hare, a symbol of fertility. She is the spirit of Spring and Her breath is in every radiant and life-bringing ray of the sun. "Bride" is a good name for Her as She is the Earth-Bride, who offers the ever renewing power of the fields to us.

Of the above description one might think that Frau Holle is a sweet lady, who wants nothing more than the best for everybody. However, She does not. Again, the double face of Fate is shown in Her seasonal aspects. Besides being the marriage-ready virgin whose perfect melody awakens the flower hidden in the dark of the Earth, She is also the Winter Goddess. She is the Winter Hag and invokes the scourging winter storms that torment the world and its inhabitants. In Her eyes you can see the ice-cold winter which kills the animals in the woods and brings starvation to the people in the villages. She is the Lady of the Wolves, who scratches at the Winter door of the hard working blacksmith. For indeed do the snowflakes fall from her sheets.

This polarity of Winter-Summer/Spring is most clearly shown in the tale of Snowwhite and Rosered. The essence of the tale is this: an old mother had two daughters, Rosered and Snowwhite. Rosered is the more 'outgoing' type, more of the flowers and happy meadows, while Snowwhite was more of the Winter and the dark, silent and melancholic indoor-crafting. Their mother always said that "what the one has, she should share with the other". They were loved by the animals of the forest, and none of whom was afraid of them nor attacked them. In the winter when snowstorms raged across Middle Earth they sat inside, spinning. They go through an initiation consisting of freeing their bear-shirt prince of the three elements, and eventually marrying him and his brother.

This is tale is full of Heathen symbolism, especially concerning the Hag-Bride polarity embedded in the image of Holle. What it comes down to is that both the seasons – Summer and Winter, symbolised by Rosered and Snowwhite – are in balance and have to share the kingdom by splitting each year in two periods of Winter and Summer. There are of course numerous other fairytales, some of which have gained quite a status thanks to Disney. One of these is the story of Snowwhite – the name keeps coming back – and of course the tale of Sleeping Beauty carries a lot of the same symbolism, though more centred around the Grail-myth and sacred kingship.

Frau Holle is the Goddess of fertility, prosperity, marriage, childbirth and Winter and Spring. Her half black face is shown in her more chthonic aspect as the Winter Goddess while Her white side is shown in Her desire to care for children and as the matron of women in want of children. If you pray to Her and bring Her offerings to increase your prosperity or fertility, you've made the right choice, for there is not a more potent Goddess you could turn to.

As Goddess of the Earth, She not only brings fertility to the fields or blesses the hardworking. Ultimately She is the patronage of woman- and especially motherhood. From Her inspiration-giving waters, children as a blessing of the Mother, are send forth. She is the matron of children, because ultimately they are Her children. She sees after them because She is their Mother, as She is the Mother of everyone. From Her Underworld womb, suited in Her Earth-body, She sends everything forth only to drag them back in, when the time comes.

The Old Goddess: Queen of the Witches

The above sounds nice and everything, but has nothing to do with us *unless* we can link Holle with Witchcraft.

Most people think of Witches as people who've sold their soul to the Devil and therefore, have to attend a Sabbath where they worship him. However, this is ridicule. Also, the Inquisitors prosecuting Witches as Devil-worshippers often had to trick/force their victims into saying that some sort of Devil was at the gatherings of Witches. Actually there wasn't such a thing, in ancient times, Witchcraft was as much known for its Goddess veneration as its nightly flights.
Frau Holle is even while mentioned several times in both Witch trials and Christian texts. Though there's much confusion about the actual name of the Witch Goddess, there is definitely enough that associates Witchcraft with Frau Holle. In parts of Germany the phrase "to ride with Holle" means exactly the same as "to ride with the Witches".

Sometimes, the Witches even got their names from Frau Holle. In the book '*Ecstasies*', by Carlo Ginzburg, he says "the Witches "venerate Her as though she were Fortune and in common parlance are called Hulden from Hulda" (pg. 94). Here, it is clearly said that the Witches were called 'Hulden', for they were followers of Hulda, Frau Holle.

The clergy had numerous names for this Goddess. These often had Latin or biblical origins such as Diana, Venus and Herodias. However, they also noted down names such as Oriente, Abundia and Sibilla. In the later editions of the texts on Witchcraft, names such as Diana in the Canon Episcopi, were replaced by "fraw Holt" or sometimes Herodias. Anyway, so many names were introduced by the clergy and the Witches themselves, that it's impossible to untwine the entire knot of confusion.

Especially in the South, the entire system of names became a mess. In the Canon Episcopi, "...*Diana, Goddess of the Pagans.."* is clearly a reference to the Wild Hunt which, on more than one occasion, was led by Frau Holle. That Witches had experiences, 'delusions', in which they travelled with the Wild Hunt and numerous trials tell us about the wide-spread survival of this cult. However, Roman tradition has *no such thing!* This leads to the conclusion that there is no way Diana could actually have been the Goddess of the Witches – at least not in the Germanic countries. Only the Germanic Goddess Holle, and the other Goddesses described as Her aspects, appears as the Mistress of the Wild Hunt.

In 1015 Holda is first mentioned by the Bishop of Worms in reference to Witchcraft, again describing the Wild Hunt. Moreover, the trial of Dian Breul in 1630, mentioned Frau Holt and Her sacred mountain, the Venusberg. In the 16th century, a woman was exiled after having confessed to have ridden with Holda's Wild Hunt.

Ultimately, she is the Goddess of Fate, the Underworld, the Earth and also the Witches. She is the chthonic deity of the Witches, and the followers of Her Cult, the people living upon the hedge, have lucid dreams in which they travel to Her dark subterranean kingdom, the Underworld. The *Hagedisse, Hagazussa* and *Hexe* take part in her good society.

the black god: death, Rebirth and the Quest for wisdom

From the last chapter, you might have gotten the impression that you have no reason to be happy about the entire Fate-issue. Probably because it interferes with our own, personal will and makes us slaves to things we cannot control. Fate continuously robs us from the pleasures of life. We strive for happiness, immortality and try to banish the pain, the darker things of life. We fear death and yet, She makes us die, we hate pain and yet, we suffer. All we want is here, however we cannot take it because were subjected to Her. In the battle of man against Fate, Fate seems to have a huge advantage and so man rarely wins. However, there are people who do win.

Now this seems a bit strange. How can one defeat an omnipotent force, a thing isn't conscious like we are? Well, "defeat" isn't the right word, it's more like "not being subject to" or "cheating" Wyrd. It means we're no longer influenced by our Fated conditions, our Fated struggle for happiness is won and She isn't able to destroy it. When this condition is reached, peace is found. You're at peace with the world, the physical for you known the inner truths and you can see the Gods shine in the world around you.

Cheating Fate is actually the same as cheating death. Death is one of those things we're *Fated* to do, and when you cheat Fate, you'll have to cheat death. You'll have to find a way to "cheat" death, twist the rules, find a maze in death's nets and turn death's inevitably into an advantage.

The Great Cheat in the Great Game

But how can one cheat death? As you know, the physical body will at some point, die and there's not much you can do about that. More likely it has to do with cheating the process of dying. But, before we can see how we can cheat death we should look into the process of death itself.

When a human being dies, his or her body stops working and slowly starts to decay. Then the personality dies too, since the body and the persona are intimately connected – the only thing remaining is some strange shade. The shade has to enter the Underworld, if not immediately after its death, it will have to someday. The dreams, memories, passions and desires, everything that defined you as you, will fade away. It dies, you will die, whether you like if or not. The ego doesn't live much longer than our prone, human bodies. However, the soul lives on.

This is probably why the dead can only be raised through magic: they've ceased to exist. Much like the dead in Greek mythology could only be re-awakened by making a blood-sacrifice, giving the soul a little bit of life-force to give it the energy so that a bit of the human personality be recovered. Raising the dead is something supernatural, for they do not exist anymore, at least not in the way we remember them.

However, in Vallhöl the dead *lived on*, they weren't forgotten. They remained conscious all the time; they still existed. The same goes for the dead in the realm of Freya and certain persons in Hel's Hall. They lived in a state of immortality, much like the Gods, only less powerful. So, we see a paradox here, people lived on forever by the favour of the Gods after they died, though in the Underworld people ceased to exist. How can this be?

This problem is solved by what Peter Paddon described in one of his podcasts as the "cosmic soup". In the cauldron we're 'recycled', but only the people who *need to be recycled*! Not everybody is recycled, because they're in that 'perfect state' already and therefore are good, perfect individuals. The rest of us: recycled.

The people who won't be recycled are a small minority, those who've done extraordinary things. Some who have done great artistic deeds and according to Norse Mythology, those who've died gloriously in battle and those who've proven to be extremely brave – not stupid though, that's something else. Those people are *granted* immortality by the Gods and so end up in the heavens with them. The rest of us? We'll have to do it the hard way.

Cheating death is quite problematic, because the only way one can NOT die is by making the physical everlasting, which isn't possible – at least not yet. More likely is that 'death' is a metaphor for something deeper. As you might have noticed in the few lines about the process of dying, the physical disintegrates and the mind does so, too. However, if one can *shift the consciousness* from the physical *to the soul*, consciousness doesn't stop at death, but lives on as long as the soul exists; which is forever.

Practically, this means death is still inevitable. However, the process of dying *can* be cheated. Normally, the human body ceases to be, leading to the following events. Firstly, the soul goes to the Underworld where the personality has to face the self or the truth, which means the end of the personality. The Ego *dies almost instantly at the moment of physical death*. Then, the consciousness is shifted from Ego to self.

This is what normally happens at death. Though, there is one way to cheat this process: facing truth/self *before* the body stops working – this will force the soul to create a new mind, only this time consciousness is rooted in the self, rather than the Ego. This is the Mystery of death & rebirth. Death is twofold disintegration; disintegration of the mind and of the body. Disintegration of the mind is something sought after by the Hedgerider, however the body is better if left intact. This means that after Rebirth, the human can take on a quite different stance on things, not always to the pleasure of the relatives and such. Though don't be afraid of losing your memory or anything like that, this is ingrained and stored in your brain which doesn't change on that point. However, the process of death & rebirth resembles a nervous breakdown, and often goes with a certain period of insanity – which is used to reintegrate the persona. This is something seen among many Shamans after their death & rebirth.

Remember the definition of 'wise' from chapter two "to experience truth"? When Fate is defeated, death is cheated; truth is found and therefore wisdom. We've defined wisdom as the constant experience of truth. Death & rebirth not only grants immortality – that is ever consciousness existence – but also wisdom and actually, these two are intimately connected.

Immortality isn't the goal here though. The Hedgerider searches after *peace* in life and the highest state of objectivity, truth. Many have said that this resembles teachings from the Buddhist Nirvana, to which it indeed shares some affinity. In the end, the Hedgerider quests after Godhead, truth and peace.

Nine Nights Upon the Tree

This symbolic death & rebirth is also found in Norse Mythology as Odin's Nine Nights Upon the Tree. In His everlasting search for wisdom, He hung himself upon the World-Tree:

> *"I hung on that windy Tree*
> *nine whole days and nights,*
> *stabbed with a spear, offered to Odin,*
> *myself to mine own self given,*
> *high on that Tree of which none hath heard*
> *from what roots it rises to heaven.*
>
> *None refreshed me ever with food or drink,*
> *I peered right down in the deep;*
> *crying aloud I lifted the Runes*
> *then back I fell from thence."*

In the first line He says that He *"hung on that windy Tree"*, which means the World-Tree, Yggdrassil. If you want to know what the

World-Tree actually stands for, take a look at the next chapter. Also note the use of *"hung"* which refers to the use of the noose and the gallows. The noose used to be the way of sacrificing victims to the old Gods, especially to Odin. Also, it was used in Traditional Witchcraft as a symbol of self-sacrifice. Actually, the Traditional Witch, Robert Cochrane, spoke of the Noose as a sacrificial tool *and* symbol.

"Nine whole days and nights". In Norse Mythology, the number nine usually reflects an unknown period, a symbolic period of initiation. Nine is not to be seen as an actual number, but more as a period or a quantity, ranging from none to infinity.

"Stabbed with a spear, offered to Odin, myself to mine own self given". These two lines are fully tied up in the death-before-you-die thing, discussed above. The spear was Odin's own weapon; meaning He killed himself. The following two lines are, however, interesting: *"offered to Odin, myself to mine own self given"*, let me just put some accents: *"my-self to mine own Self given"*. Odin slayed His ego-self for His greater self and dies while shifting His consciousness to His self. He thus turns immortal and All-wise, for He has direct experience of His self. This makes Odin wise.

"High on that Tree of which none hath heard, from what roots it rises to heaven." Again, though more clearly this time, the tree upon which Odin hung Himself is identified with the World-Tree.
"None refreshed me ever with food or drink, I peered right down in the deep; crying aloud I Lifted the Runes, then back I fell from thence." These last sentences give us a clear-cut clue about what happens when the ego-self is killed. He screamed and *"lifted the Runes"*. 'Runa' means mystery, so when he saw the Deep and found his soul, he retrieved the Mysteries from the Deep, the Underworld. He could speak the Mysteries, He could write the Mysteries and truly understand them – He had found wisdom.

Actually, death & rebirth has been part of Mystery initiations

64

all over the World. Even in British Traditional Wicca, a death & rebirth initiation is found, in the second degree to be precise. It also found in Siberian Shamanism, Freemasonry and Native American practises. It is found in the New Testament, where numerous ancient deities died and were resurrected, much like Odin.

An important thing to acknowledge is that the death & rebirth initiation is another manifestation of the Underworld journey. The journey to the Underworld is intimately connected with death and the process of death. The Hedgerider passes the same tests and perils as the dead themselves and it is likely that in the journey to the Underworld, death and rebirth are also found.

This is the reason why wisdom, the Underworld and the Hedgeriders' journey are so intimately tied up. The journey to the Underworld and death & rebirth are one and the same, deeply connected with the lore of the Hedgeriders.

Witch-Sight and Mimir's Well

Before Odin hanged himself upon the tree, He did another mysterious thing in His eternal quest for wisdom. Odin heard of the Well of Wisdom, from which a single drop would make you all-knowing. We've talked about this well earlier in Chapter One, it is also known as Mimir's Well.

The giant Mimir wouldn't let Odin drink without some sort of offering or gift. Mimir asked for Odin's eye, in return he would be able to drink from his well. So Odin would have to sacrifice his eye and therefore his ability to see depth in the physical to gain a drop from Mimir's Well and so knowledge of all things.

It is interesting to note that there's some probability of the Witches' cauldron within this Myth. In 'The Road to Hell' M.R. Ellis says that the seething cauldron (Hvergilmir), the Well of Wyrd and the Well of Mimir are one and the same. Which makes it probable that the Well of Wisdom and the Well of Wyrd were, like Hvergilmir, cauldrons; giving these wells and cauldrons an interesting death & rebirth connotation.

Again, there lies some 'Witchery' concept behind this myth. By sacrificing His worldly eye, Odin would gain insight into the truth of things, becoming wise, again. Only this time in a different sense; He sacrificed His eye to awaken His 'inner eye', as to that He could see the Godhead, the soul and the Wyrd of things. He could see the truth of Things by the awakening of His inner eye, the Eye of his soul – though not without a sacrifice.

Witches have been reputed to see the 'inner things', the dead and other such things. Mostly it is said to be clairvoyance, meaning Witches could also see the future. The ability to see the dead, see the future and see the things hidden from natural sight is often called second sight or Witch-sight and is much the same as Odin's ability to see the truth of things – it both comes down to the same.

In the Myths of Odin, there is clearly a message to humanity. I think this message screams: "WISDOM! WISDOM!" We should walk in His footsteps and search for the way of the Shaman, the way of the Sorcerer and the way of the Witch once again. We should again search for wisdom, for wisdom is what we need most. From wisdom comes clarity and peace. With these two things one can be truly happy, truly experience life in peace and happiness. Immortality? I think we can consider it a by-product, not the goal itself.

Wodan and the God of the Witches

On the continent Odin was known under a different name, Wodan, Woden, Wod, Wode etc.. His memory still continues today in the numerous towns and hills named after Him. Wodan was seen as the leader of the Wild Hunt. This tradition is still continued in the feasts of St. Nicholas in Holland, but also in the form of Santa

Claus. He still lives as Herne the Hunter, the notorious ghost of Windsor Forest.

The Wild Hunt is a procession of the dead, manifesting as dark storms roaming the midnight skies. In the winter months, when thunder scourges the land and its beings, the Wild Hunt rides across the sky, hunting after the wolf who is trying to eat the sun. This dark procession invokes dread and terror in its spectators, often causing death amongst those who watch it face to face.

The Wild Hunt can be considered an Otherworldly procession, signifying the reversal of the natural order on specified nights. The Wild Hunt was most active in the Zwölften, when the Sun had already past her lowest point. In these nights misrule ruled, the Underworld Gods installed on their Earthly Throne. For it was the in-between time, the time when the new year had not yet begun but the old one had already finished. In these nights, the door was open and the dead sat at their family's tables, eating from the Dumb Supper, the elves' Meal set aside for them. It was in these times that the people left out food and drink for the Old People, the Ancestors and the elves. Also, they would extinguish the family fire, upon which Wodan would bring the New Fire of Sunna's New Flame through the chimney, lighting the Hearth once more.

Wodan, however, also continues the cult of inspiration and death, also common in the figure of Odin. As His manifestation in the Windsor Forest, Herne the Hunter shows extremely Odinic/ Wodanic behaviour:

One day Herne was hunting with the King. In the chase of a stag, the stag turned upon them and would certainly have killed the King had Herne not taken the fatal blow. He would certainly have died, had not a local magician appeared who cured him by vesting the stag's head to Herne; in turn the King had to grant the magician his wish. Out of gratitude to Herne, the King swore to make Herne chief game keeper, if He would recover. Herne recovered and

67

returned to the castle where He was declared chief game keeper. Jealous of His great skill, the other hunters plotted against Herne. The magician, who had cured Herne, said he would take all Herne's skill, if the hunters would fulfil one of his wishes. And so it happened. Disappointed with Herne, the King banished Him from court. Herne, who was deeply hurt by the King's decision, hanged Himself from a tree.

One by one the other huntsmen were appointed chief game keeper, but once installed, they too lost their hunting skills. They went to the magician to get the problem solved. He told them to meet him at the Oak upon which Herne had hanged himself. When they appeared there, the magician told them that Herne's death was their fault, each and everyone of them and they would have to come to the Oak the next night with horses and hounds to fulfil their debt.

And so they did. When they came to the Oak, Herne appeared and made them swear an oath of allegiance to Him, they'd have to hunt with Him as their leader. Herne is said to sill hunt in Windsor forest with His pack of spectral hounds, sitting on His horse, tracking deer. Often He is depicted as a dark man with horns on His head, hunting through the forest.

You can clearly see the Wodanic/Odinic aspects of Herne; hanging Himself upon the Oak tree and His Wild Hunt through Windsor Forest. He, too, is resurrected after being hanged on a tree and leads the Wild Hunt across the sky.

Actually, Wodan survived in folk tales sometimes associated with Frau Holle and therefore, the Witches. Sometimes, it is said that He lives in the Venusberg as the benign wind-spirit, Wode, with his wife, Holda. On the continent the Witch-Mother often appears alongside Wode, suggesting that Wode could have been the master of the Sabbath.

Though the Devil appeared in a way not familiar to the Witch and was often forced upon them as an entirely foreign element, there are some things to take into account. One of the names of the Devil, Old Nick, comes from one of the names of Woden, Nikkhar. He appears as the notorious dark man, guised and cloaked with a broad rimmed hat.

Woden/Odin is famed for His hall; Vallhöl, in which the bravest of warriors lived. He was entitled to half of the slain, the other half went to Freya. One of His totem animals is the Raven, the other the Wolf, clearly associating him with the Underworld and the dead. He is the Black God.

In His black face, we can see the terror of death, for He is the terrible one, invoking dread in His enemies and followers alike. His name, Fury, is thrown across the sky when he walks the midnight skies and hunts for the souls of the dead. He is the door into the Underworld, for His terror is the terror of death itself and in His black face this is reflected.

Also, pure rage and fury are expressed in His wild heirs, the furious host. Even His name bears out this meaning. He was the God of the Warriors, of the Berserker who went to fight in ecstatic frenzy, which gives us another meanings of Him: ecstasy, trance. He was the God of – poetic – inspiration & wisdom, and ecstasy.

As the Black Master, the God of Wisdom, He shows us the path of the Hedgerider; the way of the wise people. When His ecstasy is invoked, the spirit is released and can be sent forth into the dark of night and the Hedgerider can go and ride with the furious host of Frau Holle. As God of Wisdom, He has shown the Way of wisdom, the way of death & initiation. Ultimately, he is the great Ancestor of the Hedgepath.

Steeds & Stangs:
Initiating Trance and
Witch-Sight

In the last Chapters, the World-Tree has been mentioned a few times without a full explanation. The World-Tree is a giant Ash or Yew – it's not entirely clear – upon which the nine worlds of Norse Mythology are vested. The Underworlds lie between the roots while Midgard is suited in the middle of the trunk, the heavens lie at the top, the crown of the World-Tree. Between these three 'levels' the World-Tree works as a medium by which all the worlds are connected and can be entered. The roots lie above the Well of Wyrd, from which the World-Tree drinks.

The World-Tree is called Yggdrasill and is sometimes referred to as Mimameid. Yggdrasill means "terrible" (ygg) + "steed" (drasil). 'Terrible' is a name for Odin, meaning that Yggdrasill is called "Odin's Steed". Mimameid means Mimir's tree, meaning it's the tree of the giant who heeded the Well of Wisdom and again refers to the connotation between the Well of Wisdom and the origins of the World-Tree.

The Wooden Steed and the Pole

This might seem a bit strange: how can a tree, especially such a large tree, be a steed, a horse? The tree-steed should not be taken literally, but rather as a symbol, a euphemism for a sorcerous concept. Some people have suggested that the World-Tree is called Yggdrasill, because Odin hanged Himself upon this tree. However, this doesn't explain why it's called a *steed*, a horse that is ridden. The Steed of Odin is actually a magical horse, Sleipnir. Sleipnir was the horse that carried Odin into the Underworld, as well as other people in other stories. Sleipnir is a magical vehicle by which Odin and other Gods could cross the boundary and enter Hell. In this light, the idea of the World-Tree as a steed isn't that strange anymore. The World-Tree was used as a *medium,* the pole that connected the worlds. By riding this tree, Odin or any other Hedgerider, could go into the Underworld.

Actually, wooden poles ridden in the fashion of a horse are quite common in Witchery. A matter of fact is that Witches rode the Broom when leaving for the Sabbath. Though the Broom doesn't really resemble a pole, there is definitely something there. Actually, the Witches didn't ride the Broom. In earlier times, they had some other strange vehicle, much more like a pole. This is called the 'Stang'. The Stang resembles the wooden pitchfork and is not only an agricultural tool, but also a vehicle of transportation for the Witches. The word 'Stang' comes from the Old Norse word for pole, but also means 'ladder' in one of the English dialects. The 'ladder' meaning is actually quite interesting, as it suggests that the Stang is a *ladder into the Otherworlds*.

The last meaning dedicates a lot of importance to the fact that Witches rode Stangs. I suggest you take a look at the appendix to see some of the paintings depicting Witches sitting on Stangs.
The phrase 'riding the Stang' refers to a practice known as the Skimmington Ride, which is a ritual by which criminals, usually wife-beaters, were punished by social humiliation. It was common throughout England, but died out in the 19th century due to industrialization.

What happened during this strange form of social punishment was that the violator had to ride the Stang and was, for a short period, ritually exiled. This however takes us back to the practice of crossing the hedge as the boundary between the wild and civilization.

In chapter one, riding the Stang would denote the breaking of the cultural boundary, which is the Underworld boundary: "*They cross the hedge, which is, among other things, the boundary between the Wild and the Civilized.*" The punishment of exile into the Underworld – meaning the ban from the protection of the Law – was actually a common practice in Northern regions. In this ritual, the Stang is used as a vehicle for exile or the journey into the Underworld – signifying that the violator is considered 'wolf-like' and dishonourable – this would mean a deep association between

73

the Stang and the Underworld journey This, again, gives meaning to the rites of the Witches as rites of Underworld travelling.

Actually, the Stang was still used in ritual by the Traditional Witch Robert Cochrane, who claimed a hereditary line running through his family. He and his group, the Clan of Tubal-Cain, enacted rituals in which the Stang was considered the door, or 'Malkuth', into the Otherworld and also symbolized the Master's presence as Horned God of death and terror – He being the door to the Underworld. This resembles much of the rites of Freyr. In these rites a Stang – a piece of wood with antlers vested on top – was erected. Anyway, in traditional Witch-rites, the Stang is seen as the representation of the dark God, who is the gate to Hell.

Trance: Yggdrasill, the Stang and the Medium of Flight

According to lore, Brooms and Stangs are both made of Ash, suggesting a connection with Yggdrasill. More importantly though, they are the vehicle of transportation to the Sabbath. The Stang or the Broom was anointed with flying ointment and was then 'ridden' while the Hedgerider was naked. This enabled the hallucinogenic alkaloids to be absorbed into the body, initiating a sensation of flying. Then the Witch took off to the land of the elves, flying on the Stang – this is again shown in the paintings.
The Stang here is ridden in the same fashion as the World-Tree by Odin. Yggdrasill as a pole however, has much symbolism attached to it. The World-Tree/Stang is the medium of flight, the experience *invoking* the Underworld experience.

The World-Tree can be seen as that which connects all worlds, a reality or state of being which connects all the worlds. When Odin rides his steed, he takes part in this reality and invokes this state of being by which he can access all the worlds. This is much like the oracular state in which the Völva of several Scandinavian Saga's find themselves; a state in which they can access the worlds and the flow of Wyrd. The state of being in which Odin is when he rides the World-Tree is the state of Wyrd, soul, Godhead: this state of being is called trance.

Trance is the medium of flight, the expansion of awareness that enables the Hedgerider to engage in Otherworldly activities – the state of being in which the Hedgerider can ride the Stang – in which Odin can access the Underworld. Trance is symbolized by the Stang and in a certain sense, the horse. Often these are employed to invoke its mystical clarity.

Remember me talking about the 'permanent experience of Godhead' and the 'heart of your strand', the 'inner reality of this world'? Trance is the experience of this. It's like a drop from Mimir's Well – the key to Witch-sight and seeing the truth of things. It's the riding of the Stang, the experience of the World-Tree.

It is in this state of unification of the worlds that the Underworld can be accessed. It is by riding the World-Tree, the steed-Stang, that trance is invoked. This is seen in the riding of the Broom by the Witches. They ride the Stang before they enter the Underworld – actually the Witches' journey resembles important elements from the Norse conception of the Underworld journey.

HedgeWitche's core practice is centered around the Underworld journey and therefore, around the invoking of trance. There is NO WAY you can enter the Underworld without the alteration of your consciousness, for you will have to experience the inner to access the Underworld. That alteration is done by trance – it is the experience of the inner – without the key of trance, the door will stay fully locked. And so if you want to be a HedgeWitch you need to know how to invoke trance.

The Practice of Invoking Trance

As you might expect, the invocation of trance isn't without danger and is especially hard on the ego-fixed mind. So there should be a warning here: I'm not telling you to do this. It is your own choice, your own responsibility and I tell you to watch out and to be VERY CAREFUL in what you do and try to do, and I suggest you DO NOT do it.

The basic effect of trance is that there's an expansion of awareness, not only do you experience your body, but you also experience the world around you, though not necessarily in the same manner. Also, you'll notice that the world around you and the way you perceive it, becomes much, much more clear. It is as if you've always had your sunglasses on your nose and suddenly take them of – everything becomes clear. Also, there are trances which can be described as 'hallucinogenic' in the sense that strange beings are encountered and the physical world seems 'stretched' or 'bent' or entirely different, filled with the most curious spirits and beings. Often these trances are the product of actual hallucinogenic substances.

There are several ways to go about invoking trance; although every technique has its own advantages and disadvantages and every technique is different they can roughly be divided in three categories:

    i. The use of herbal substances/entheogens
    ii. Mind-based techniques
    iii. Physical action

When applied these become:

    i. Flying ointment, incense and (alcoholic) liquids
    ii. Simple visualization, pathworkings and concentration, imagination, lucid dreaming etc..
    iii. Ritual, riding the Broom, the Witches' dance etc..

Obviously, the first and the third are often mixed since herbal substances can more easily be applied when they are incorporated in physical ritual. Also, ritual and techniques of the mind are often mixed, producing rituals that rely heavily on location, such as an Otherworldly gate, and the technique to open the door and walk through it.

First, we'll be discussing the use of herbal substances, then we'll go into the mind-based techniques. In the meantime, I'll be discussing some crossovers and combined techniques. The last, ritual, will be incorporated into the last Chapter mixed with some history and important lore – which you'll find in the other Chapters as well – the rituals you'll encounter as the Spell of the Wolf and the Spell of the Hawthorn. However, it is beyond the scope of this book to discuss all the rituals of Hedge Witchery.

Entheogens

The Hedgeriders have employed so called 'flying ointments' which consisted of some kind of fat or oil and several heavily poisonous herbs and plants such as wolfbane, yew, deadly nightshade etc.. The exact method of preparation is, however, lost and how they did it is still a bit of a mystery. The chemicals inside the plants should be mixed in exact the right measures or the poisonous alkaloids will kill you. However, it is impossible to tell how much of a certain chemical a plant contains. Due to different conditions, the content of a plant can vary widely. To balance the equation without the traditional knowledge of the old days is impossible and to reconstruct a properly working flying ointment and to apply it to your skin is extremely dangerous. Though today, there are several known methods to induce trance by the aid of herbal substances which are often more safe than say... tobacco.

If these methods are known and available to us, then we should ask ourselves the important question: should we use it? When people talk about these matters they usually talk about 'drugs' and 'addiction', 'rehab', 'jail' etc.. However, so called 'entheogens' are still applied in certain Traditional Witch-groups. Entheogen means 'bringing forth the God' and is the name used for herbal substances that are used for spiritual and/or magical purposes. The important thing to remember is that entheogens are *rarely used for recreational purposes*. Not because they have limited effect, but because they aren't really 'fun' – it takes a lot of time and discipline to really establish an effective state of mind. Often, they only enhance your mood or the state you're in, making it for the 'normal' recreational user, not really that exciting.

Also important: it's legal. In most countries, hard drugs – drugs that pose a threat to your health, like cocaine, heroine, crack, crystal meth etc.. are all illegal and should be, I think. However, the more benign 'soft drugs' – drugs that pose no disproportional threat to your health – like marihuana and magic mushrooms are also illegal in most countries. In Holland, the distinction between soft-drugs and hard-drugs is made and therefore soft-drugs are available in certain shops. Interestingly enough, the use of both hard- and soft-drugs is significantly lower than in other countries. Anyway, I think that in the application of herbal substances we should make the same distinction: harmful entheogens are to be left alone while the benign ones are available for use – if they're legal of course.

That's actually an important criterion: the legality of your actions. Though there are a hundred reasons why the government is wrong, it is still the Law and you don't want to end up in jail because you thought that a good Witch-ritual asked for some nice, hallucinogenic mushroom which happened to be illegal. ALWAYS make sure that what you are doing is LEGAL.

Safety is another important issue. There are several things you have to check before you can even think about the use of an entheogen. One: your allergies. If you turn out to have some strange allergy against mugwort or wormwood or whatever, you'll get yourself in a terrible mess. Also make sure that you're using no medication, because the things you use will be unconventional and so the doctors will not have tested the medicine combined with some strange plant. So if you're allergic or under medication, do NOT try it – generally don't try it.

What you also have to take into consideration is that you probably don't know what kind of effect the entheogen will have upon you. So what you need is someone with you who doesn't take part in the substance and can help you if something goes wrong. Mandatory: this person should be an experienced practitioner and should have traditional knowledge about herbs and especially the plant you will be using. I think this is the biggest obstacle for most people, since there aren't that many people around who know about entheogens and even less people who will teach you. But trust me; you really, really don't want to do this without an experienced person by your side.

About the Spirit of the Plant

Now, after all the safety warnings we can get back to business. You know which herb you want to use. You've researched it and know everything there is to know about it. Also, you have somebody with you who has done it before and will be your guardian for the night. The only thing left is to collect the plant and then prepare it so that it may be useful. Collecting a plant, i.e. the taking of life is a delicate issue in Witchery. Remember that everything is alive? You're ending life and that – according to the workings of Fate – will have to be balanced by something else. You kill something and Wyrd wants a piece of you instead. Basically this means you have to make some sort of offering. Usually, this consists of a libation of red wine poured on the ground or a piece of bred blessed in the Old One's name and left at the place where the root of the plant once was. Sometimes the life you end, the power you take is greater and especially if you have to ingest a plant, you want to let it be 'alive' and full of spirit so that it will work with you. If this is the case you'll have to make a blood sacrifice. Now don't think that's 'evil' or 'wicked' or 'satanic', because it's not – in fact the entire Old Testament is full of blood sacrifice. What I mean is that when you take a life, you have to pay your respects and have to balance the flow of Wyrd: you have to give something back. Nothing is more symbolic or more powerful than a drop of blood. I'm not suggesting that you should cut off your hand – an anonymous new ager: "but the tree is sacrificing a arm too!" – That's ridiculous. Just take a needle and pierce your skin and anoint the tree with the blood coming from the little wound. Then, just take the part of the plant that you need.

I cannot say I have tried all the recipes described hereunder and have relied upon other peoples' experiences with them. Don't interpret this information as a 'how-to' guide, but as information that can guide you through the realms of misinformation and such.

Now you're ready for the actual recipes and preparation methods. First, I will be discussing the entheogens with the least potency and then I will go into the more effective ones. And let me remind you: don't do anything stupid.

Wine: an Entheogen

Although you might not expect 'alcohol' to be a entheogen, it can be usefully employed within ritual and spiritual practice. Even the Gardnerian Book of Shadows mentions 'drugs, alcohol and incense' as one of the eight paths to magical power. Also, wine is used in the traditional Christian Mass and also in the Witches' Houzle – which looks much like the Christian Mass, or rather the Christian Mass looks much like the Houzle. Today, ale or mead is a favored drink by Heathens and Druids alike, often giving a certain oldness, a feeling of 'bonding' made by drinking what our Ancestors drank. Of course, ale is also used in the Heathen's 'symbel' – a toast in which the Heathen thanks the Gods and boasts about what he has accomplished.

The effects of alcohol are, when employed as 'just' a drink, not of much use and the worst it will do is make you drunk and give a terrible hangover the next day – nothing mystical about that. However, if you are disciplined enough, a combination of certain physical actions and the right dose will bring you terrific results.

First, you should NOT do this if you're an alcoholic or have a past of alcohol abuse and/or addiction or if you're under age. The spiritual use of alcohol in our modern society is quite a problem, since it immediately is associated with 'parties' and 'getting drunk' and such; while the ritual employment of wine requires quite a disciplined mind. The use of alcohol in a ritual setting is often in small, very small amounts and wouldn't even get you tipsy if you just drink it in front of your TV.

There's not much too it, actually. The key is to create an atmosphere of 'ritual', of 'darkness' – simply the association with the Old God, the Black God. Imagine a hilltop, surrounded by large woods in which you can hear the wolves howl and you can almost see the Witches fly over the hills. A fire lights the first two meters, you can't look any further. Behind the fire stands a Stang, fully cloaked and with a skull vested between the horns. Everything is creepy and it feels as if you're walking around on a forgotten, half-ruined cemetery – anything can happen. That's the atmosphere you need to create! A feeling that the world isn't logical anymore; a world where the physical isn't stable and everything is full of spirit, as if the dead can rise up and walk through your bedroom. Order is gone and it's just you and the spirits.

What helps me is the flickering of candles and the smell of some strange incense. What might also help is the use of ritual garments and robes – anything that 'turns you on' and gets you into that half-excited, half-frightened state. Some Witches like to prance around naked, some just use entheogens to get to that state, some think of their mum – just kidding. Anything goes.

So, you're in a circle of candles and incense drifts through the forgotten cottage you're sitting in, now you have to take the alcohol. Here comes the big issue, because everybody has different habits –

especially when it comes to drinking – it is quite difficult to decide how much you have to take. I suggest you're not drinking more than one beer, because if you do you'll have to walk or crawl home. The best alcoholic liquid for ritual employment is the famous red wine. Because of the quite high alcohol percentage – 14 to 16 percent – you don't have to drink large amounts, but your intestines won't get burned away – which often happens when you get closer to the 20%. Begin with a small dose, one sip will do. You just sit around and can try to use one of the trance techniques discussed at the end of this chapter and every ten minutes you take another sip. You *keep on doing* this until you're in a perfect meditative state – without, of course, crossing the limits of alcohol-poisoning and any legal or health limit. I must say that the trance springing from the use of alcohol can effectively be employed to raise 'a cone of power'. Wild, ecstatic dancing is also used as a magical tool within Traditional Witchcraft. Often, the Stang is used a mediator and is thus placed in the center, then you start to dance, clockwise or anti-clockwise, whatever suits you – personally I don't believe it really matters. You run your guts out and when you can no longer take it, you focus on your target and drop down, still focusing strongly on the 'target'.

Some people use alcohol in combination with the deprivation of food or *fasting* – actually several sorts of deprivation are used to induce trance and spirit-vision. They simply stop eating for a day or eat very little and then in the night, when the bells mark the Witching hour, they start the rite.

The Witching Hour is often equated with midnight and the first hour of the morning, the thirteen hour. It is the 'in-between time' when the gates between the middle and the under are open and the elf-spirits walk the Earth. Some traditions say it is midnight, others think of it as the time between day and night, dusk and dawn. Also mist or fog is considered to be Otherworldly in nature – remember Niflheim, mist-heim?

Back to the method of fasting. It's not a really nice or easy-going method and will require you to dedicate an entire day to the induction of trance – which of course is what every Witch wants, *if* they have the time. Anyway, the method most used is to not have breakfast and only drink water. If the lunch approaches you start to eat little things like fruit and start to drink more and more. Actually, fruits are very favourable, because they are digested very well and are almost entirely converted into energy reserves ready to be used. You eat nothing until the rite, which will get you – eventually – into a state of half-trance and when you employ the wine, it will come on twice as powerful making the trance more visual.

Mugwort & Wormwood

Mugwort *(Artimisia Vulgaris)* is known under several names such as common wormwood, wild wormwood and St. John's Plant – not to be confused with St. John's Wort. The plant grows quite high, about one to two meters and is often considered a 'weed'. It grows along roadsides, train tracks and abandoned ground. Mugwort is a so called 'pioneer plant' which means it's one of the first plants to grow on an empty piece of ground, often appearing alongside thistle.

The twin of mugwort is wormwood *(Artimisia Absinthium)* which looks much like mugwort, only the leaves are more round, instead of the sharp points of Vulgaris and the flowers are yellow. Anyway, I suggest you use a good herbal to identify them properly, as there are several plants that look like them.

Both species are extremely useful when it comes to invoking trance, lucid dreaming, oracular workings, ancestral workings, poetry and spirit flight. On the bad side: they are poisonous. The active ingredient being responsible for the useful effects is called thujon ($C_{10}H_{16}O$) mythic for its poison – though recent studies counter this. Thujon is one of the active chemicals in the drink

Absinth which is currently illegal in the US, Canada and the UK. Interestingly enough, it's way less poisonous than assumed by the authorities. Recent studies have proven that Absinth isn't disproportionally dangerous, because of this Absinth was legalized in the Netherlands.

There is actually some interesting lore attached to both of the Artimisia's. The name 'artimisia' comes from the Goddess Artimis – the Greek counterpart of Diana. She was the Goddess of hunting, the moon, wild animals and was considered the Goddess of the Witches by the medieval and renaissance clergy. The Romans themselves related mugwort to Diana, whose totems – goats and rams – prefer the stems and leaves of *vulgaris*.

Although mugwort is strongly connected with the southern Goddesses, it is also strongly connected with the northern Goddess, Frau Holle. In the German tongue, mugwort, when culinary applied, is called 'goose-wort'. Mother Goose is a name of the Witchmother and geese are considered the totem of Hedge Witchery and spirit flight.

Northern European Shamans used to sacrifice a goose to the nature spirits who would retreat to their homes until the next Spring. They rubbed the goose with mugwort and then used the fat of the goose to make the notorious flying ointment. The Shamanic elements embedded within this rite and the obvious connection between mugwort and geese – indirectly connects it to Mother Goose and spirit flight.

Before we get to the practical application of mugwort and wormwood – which can be used interchangeably, only the dose can vary – we'll have to talk about safety, again. I'm sorry and you probably don't want to hear this over and over again, but I just can't get around the safety warnings. Thujon is *poisonous* and can be considered *dangerous* and even *lethal* when overdosed. So, stick to the described dose and don't over-dose – you'll just end up in a nasty place, like the hospital.

The simplest way to employ both the Artemisia's is by making a tea. Just take a couple of dried leaves, cut them into small pieces and throw it in half a liter of boiling water. Half a liter might be a bit much to drink, so you can just switch the water quantities. An important thing to remember is that the only way you'll really extract some of the chemicals is by boiling the leaves. Boil it for 2-5 minutes and after the tea turns greenish, it will get a golden/yellow glow, then you know it is ready.

Although this is the easiest way ,it sure has a lot of disadvantages. First there is the taste – it tastes really, really bitter and drinking it is a very unpleasant experience, especially when you use wormwood. Also the boiling-process is difficult to incorporate into ritual, unless you have a cauldron, and since the most useful effects happen somewhere between 10 to 20 minutes after ingestion, making a tea is quite difficult. Smoking is another alternative but that leaves you with the health-risks from tobacco. If you have no problem with smoking, this is probably the easiest way to go about it. Just cut the mugwort into very small pieces. The best time to do this is when it's still fresh, although some of the potentiality is lost , it becomes way smaller which is preferable. I suggest you use mugwort, absinthium means 'distasteful', even if it just touches your lips. Roll it up with tobacco and inhale. You'll notice that the effects come in way faster tha with the tea, probably within the space of 5 minutes.

Then, there's the possibility of making an ointment. The application of ointments is harder, but way more symbolic and beautiful when it comes to ritual. Some people have problems with applying the ointment to the skin and this method doesn't seem to be as potent, compared to the other two. However, there are some solutions to this. One of these comes close to one of the Gardnerian eights paths of magic; the scourge. More accurately put, this is the path of blood control and that is exactly what we need here. Before you

rub the ointment on your skin you can use a nine-knotted cord
– *cingulum* in some traditional groups – to heighten the content
of blood within certain parts of you body where you'll apply the
ointment. The best place to rub the ointment is at the wrist and
some also say the soles of your feet or sometimes at the top of your
foot. Also flagellation can be used to 'activate' the skin and irritate
it a bit so that the ointment will be absorbed faster into the blood
stream.

Making the ointment is quite simple, all you have to do is take a
few centililiters of olive oil – the best you can find and then take
the dried herbs and toss them into the ointment. The good thing
about this ointment is that it's really hard to overdose. The exact
recipe is this:

1	part wormwood
¾	part mugwort
1½	part holy herb
1¼	part silverweed

Dry it for at least two weeks, preferably near a hearth and then cut
it fine or crumble it over the olive oil. Additionally, you can add
some ash of a fire used to burn mugwort or wormwood. Let all this
stand in a closed jar for a month, or maybe two and when the clear
greenish color of olive oil is lost, turned distinctly darker, isn't that
clear and more thick, you know it's ready.

Both the artimisia's give you a very 'clear' state of mind and you'll
get the instant urge to be creative. The drink absinth which is made
out of wormwood is said to be responsible for most of Van Gogh's
art – it's just a myth, but indeed gives you a hint about the creative
side of this entheogen. It is often employed in oracular workings,
especially when it comes to recovering ancestral lore but also in the
praxes of shape shifting. The ointment described above especially
helps when it comes to spirit flight and sending forth the Fetch,
also known as 'astral travel'. One of the most curious properties

is that mugwort can be used to invoke lucid dreams. If you drink some of the tea before you go to sleep, or put a handful of leaves under your pillow, your dreams will become very 'alive' and you will be able to act as you would in the everyday world. This can both be exciting and fearful, because it also *feels* as the everyday world – what if a nightmare would feel real? Anyway, you will be able to remember your dreams. I warn you however, the dreams aren't always nice.

Sweet Flag

Calamus (*Acorus Calamus*), also known as common sweet flag or myrtle grass is a plant which originally comes from India and now grows throughout Europe, southern Russia, southern Siberia, China, Japan, Burma, Sri Lanka and the USA.

The trance-state that sweet flag induces is especially good for what has been called 'ecstatic workings'. Often rising some sort of sexual energy, it is most effectively employed in the ring-dances of the Witches. The use of physical movements is very important when applying this herb. What is basically done is that a pole, Broom or Stang is erected in the middle and the Witches start to dance around it, often pointing with their left hand at the pole. Then a vortex is raised in the middle of the circle of dancing Witches. From this vortex, the unseen Powers come forth. A gate-way is created by the stirring and conscious application of the fetch-power and the left-hand, left-way symbolism. Alternatively, a cauldron filled with blessed water from a natural source or sometimes red wine, is placed in the middle and after the raising of the vortex, one of the Witches kneels down, seeing the visions of the unseen in the mirror-like surface of the liquid.

This trance state can also effectively be used in the so called 'raising the fire' or 'raising the serpent'. Because of the arousal of sexual energy and the alchemical process attached to this, the fire or serpent thought to 'live' inside the spine can be raised.

The sparks inside the belly can be used to fan the flames inside the spine by what is called the 'breath of the bellows'. Imagine that the world around you is one great bellow and sucks the air out of your lungs when you exhale and pushes it in when you inhale. Your body will start to 'move', to really 'feel' this process of inhaling and exhaling. Then the breath of the bellows is used to fan the flame higher and higher; when you get it right, you can feel serpent winding around your spine.

The application of the sweet flag ointment is especially good when combined with the ecstatic raising of the Fetch and so the induction of shape-shifting. Instead of remaining in a passive state, as induced by the mugwort ointment, this ointment will urge you to move, dance and chant. It is much like the 'animal dance' of the Shaman; you start to dance, run around the scene and move like the animal moves. Slowly, you'll start to identify with it, raising the frightening power of it and then you can project your consciousness into it, completing the shape shifting.

The most commonly used part, when it comes to entheogens, is the dried root. Sweet flag can be employed in two ways: i) in a tea ii) in an ointment. The tea is the easy method; all you have to do is take 2-3 teaspoons of the dried root – which is available in most stores carrying herbs, or through the internet – and add it to boiling water. Let it boil for 2-3 minutes and then take it off the fire and let it soak for a minute or two. Additionally, one could add some hops which is said to strengthen the tea and intensify the experience.

According to some sources, sweet flag is one of the ingredients of the notorious drink 'absinth', which we already talked about in the section about mugwort & wormwood. For an extra effect you could add sweet flag and hyssop to your artimisia-tea. Also, adding calamus to the ointment can sometimes be considered a good idea if you're looking for a more 'ecstatic' experience.

Making an ointment out of sweet flag isn't too difficult. Add 3-5 teaspoons of calamus to 40 ml olive oil, and let it soak for a couple of months. You can also add some mugwort (1/4), hyssop, also 3-5 teaspoons and some St. Johns wort, 2 teaspoons.

Passionflower

Passionflower (*Passiflora Incarnata*) is a plant from South-America and was first brought to Europe as a gift for the Pope. The name Passiflora Incarnata refers to the passion of Christ, the shape of the flower is thought to resemble several elements of Christ's death and resurrection.

Though it's not common for Witches to use entheogens from other cultures, the passionflower can prove extremely useful. As you might have noticed, the entheogens are discussed in order of potency, and this one is last for several reasons. The trance induced by the passionflower is very useful when employed in combination with a technique that is known as 'pathworking' – which isn't the same as a guided meditation. The passionflower really focuses the mind upon one thing and aids the concentration. It enables you to focus the mind, but also it 'enlivens' the visualized surroundings and almost makes them real.

The easiest way to employ passionflower is through a tea. Just take some dried passionflower, especially the leaves, and boil it for 1 to 2 minutes, then take it of the fire and let it soak for another two minutes. Add 2-4 teaspoons, if you add more it will lead to hallucinations and loss of reality. The dosage you add to the boiling water is key, as too much may cause serious trouble. Passionflower slows down the enzymes working on the poison in ordinary food between the synapses of your nervous system. Anti-depressants and other medicines can become extremely dangerous when combined with passionflower, for they are allowed to constantly work upon the body. I advice you to first consult your personal physician before you try it – or anything else. Moreover, to avoid nausea and headaches do NOT eat 12 hours – preferably more – before employing passionflower.

Passionflower can also be smoked, which will shorten the experience to a more acceptable length, usually 20-30 minutes instead of a full hour. When smoked, it is easier to determine the dose, especially if you wait for 5 minutes after every stick so you really know when it kicks in. You might want to add skullcap and damiana to your mixture, this will produce a marihuana-like high which can be used for oracular purposes and ancestral-oracular workings. Of course, this works as well when you add it to your tea – keep the dose 1/1/1.

Because of the effects of passionflower on the nervous system, it is also employed by recreational users to enhance the effect of mushrooms. The small amount of DMT is activated through the slower process between the synapses, this intensifies the experience severely. I, however, do NOT advise you to use mushrooms, not even the 'shrooms' which are relatively safe, and I definitely stress you NOT to use one of the more poisonous species like fly agaric. Though these might have been used in the past and are intimately connected with the elffolk, the journey to the Sabbath and the Shamanic rites of the Hedgerider, I advise you not to: you'll only end up hurt or in a hospital.

Spirit or Mind-Based Techniques

We've extensively discussed the use of entheogens, making some side trips into the rituals and techniques of traditional Witches. Though now, I think, we should discuss the second of the three 'ways' of invoking trance and Underworld contact: spirit techniques. These techniques are based upon the power of the mind and rely most importantly upon *suggestion* and autosuggestion. Remember though that the suggestion often is used to release the mind of its boundaries, making it capable of perceiving more layers of reality. The biggest part of these techniques relies upon the individual's own discipline and condition and, of course, constant repetition. Even more than with the uses of entheogens, spirit techniques rely upon the individual's discipline, nothing else.

Some notes made should be that the following techniques are *only samples*, things I've found to work and they are definitely not *the* way to achieve trance. Many people have their own way(s) of achieving trance, some like to glare at a candle, others retrace certain symbols with their fingers; all that loosens the mind is acceptable.

Awakening of Awareness

This technique bases itself upon the idea that All is One. By the expansion of self to All, trance is thought to be conceived. It is also known as "Lying on the Land", which, quite descriptively, states what this technique is all about.

Before you begin, you really have to focus and be able to hold that focus for at least fifteen minutes. Having read this book so far, I think you are very well capable of that; this actually goes for every way of invoking trance. Find someplace quiet, where you can be without being disturbed. The key is to find a place where you can make contact with the earth, the land. On this place you have to lie down, thinking about the powers in the deep below. Then, when you are lying comfortable and find yourself focussed upon the Underworld, you concentrate upon the land beneath, how it touches your skin, the small bumps and holes, the stones and the vast darkness beneath you. You think only about that, focus all your senses upon it, upon the ground beneath you. See the Earth, feel the Earth and yes, even hear the Earth – that's the key; realizing it is alive and aware.

It might take several times before you will succeed, though in the end you will have a deep connection, a deep share of awareness with the living Earth. Your senses will have expanded inward, to the inner, in both ways.

The core of this technique is the focussing of the senses. You have to open up, really open up to the Power in the Land, and direct your mind towards it. You have to shut down all your thoughts and concentrate your full being into the Land – that's the key.

This technique can be used really well with the use of the ointments already described. I suggest the mugwort-base ointment to enhance the clarity in your mind. Also, I suggest you use this technique as the starting point of your practice and you should use it before every attempt at Witchery.

Pathworking

Pathworking is a technique relying upon what is known as "visualisation". It is centred around the picturing of images to the mind – rather than to the senses – and by these, bringing about a subtle change in perception. Of the practitioner it requires a rather good concentration and certainly a great level of imagination.

Close your eyes, leave the world while you don't think about a thing. You can start by picturing yourself in a meadow, or a forest or the backyard. You must almost be able to touch the grass, feel the stones and smell the trees. At first everything will seem very 'imagined', as if it weren't real. The longer you practice and try, the longer you walk around, things will starting to become even more real. You will have to continue to walk around and act until the world you're in becomes as real as the most vivid dream you've had; as vivid as life is. Actually, this technique is a way of invoking a lucid dream, which is a dream in which you can act and decide upon your own. When you're capable of walking around, seeing things as if they exist, you can go to the 'next level'.

You're in a dark, old forest and stand upon a small road which leads you to a small meadow. Before you, there is a huge mountain wall, reaching 50 metres into the sky. At eye level there is a cave, the darkness lures you while you stand before it. At the sides, you notice, there are certain runes and symbols carved into the mountain. You are lured into the darkness, bringing it closer to you – but not too close! – and you dwell upon it, thinking about what might be in there. And you think and watch, think and watch, until the subtle trance state of Elf-Land is reached.

Of course, the above is just an example and is only a rough outline of what it should be. However, the key in this technique is that it's not you who makes things happen, the things make *themselves happen!* You just sit and wait, staring at the cave, well, stone, tree, stag, wolf, bear, boar, owl, grave-mound, hill, whatever feature you think will bring about the desired change in perception.

Other methods have you visualize symbols and watching them, contemplating about them. To the Heathens among us, these symbols are obviously the runes, though some Hedgerider use specific Witch-symbols more attached to their own tradition.

Though most people will immediately think of a so called 'guided meditation' when reading the above, it is far from it. The point is that this technique is definitely *not* a guided meditation, because it isn't guided. Nobody is telling you what to do or what to see, it all happens out of yourself – and therefore the above is only a example of what might happen. You can just explore the road and be content with what's there.

With the above however, there's one think to take into account when trying this technique. The idea is that you're trying to create a loosening of the mind as to find the root within yourself by which you can experience All. This means there's going to be a sharpening of the perception of the Witch-sight, which can lead to the lessening of the physical sight and experience. In fact, this technique can lead to the loss of sense, full experience of the inner and an expansion of consciousness – which can be dangerous or difficult in normal, everyday action.

Serpent Swaying

This technique centres around the arousal of the fire and serpent thought to live in the spine. Robert Cochrane equated this concept with the Eastern idea of 'Kundalini'. Of old, the serpent has been a symbol of wisdom and the Underworld – Wyrmsele, remember? The serpent curls around the spine and can be aroused by the breath. It is believed that by the breath the Ancestral fire can be fanned into a higher flame, invoking the Swaying of the Serpent.
In the last chapter, we'll deal more extensively with the Ancestral fire, though for the sake of logical order I'll shortly discuss it here. The Ancestral fire is the sacred fire, which is thought to have been given to humanity by the Witch-God shortly after the beginning – this is the fire of culture, art, reason etc.. The Ancestral fire is that quality which separates us from animals – animals aren't less because of this though. Anyway, the Ancestral fire is believed to be the 'gnostic base' of the Old Ways, initiating the Old Ways over and over again in those people who can be trusted to guard it. This is what is called 'Godly transmission' or 'personal gnosis' discussed in Traditional Witchcraft and is that what separates the wannabe's from the true Witches.

Anyway, the fanning of this sacred flame opens you up to the Godly Beings and your own soul. What is important in this rite, is that you have some sort of fire which you can use as a reflection of your own flame. The key here is that you are in control of your breath and are able to direct it, slow it down and speed it up by command. You begin by lighting the candle, a pile of wood or lamp and you sit in front of it. As the fire starts to rise, your breath slows down, inhaling for about 5 seconds and keeping it in for another 5 seconds – if this is too long you will notice, instead of relaxing your heart will speed up! When you've inhaled for about 20/25 times, lean forward to the fire and try to inhale the spirit of the fire. With all your force you inhale, slowly exhale and again you powerfully inhale and slowly exhale – you let the rhythm of the fire take over and let it go as fast as it wants you to. Now, you should be noticing a strange effect, a strange feeling in the lower parts of your stomach, this is what is called the 'Stirring of the Serpent'. Slowly, this feeling will start to move upwards, along your spine. What might help is to slowly let the air slip between your teeth, the serpent's hiss. When the serpent reaches the skull, trance is conceived along with Ancestral inspiration.

Chanting

Personally I'm really not into singing, but for you, my reader, I will make an exception and talk about it. The pronunciation of certain sacred vowels or sentences can lead to the desired shift in consciousness. This mainly goes by the idea that sound is all-penetrating and so passes all layers of Fate and existence. It is the sending out of "vibrations" which lead to a desired change in the world. In the Norse areas, the use of chants was considered to be magic and the name for a Magus was among others, 'song-man'.
The point is, how can we find the vowels that induce a desired change? Well, I think we should take a look at the lore we've already turned to for many, many answers: Norse Mythology. In the study of the runes, there's a real possibility, especially since every rune has its own word and correspondence, which could give you the excellent opportunity to find out how to 'sing magic'. So the vowels associated with the runes can be used as a chant, especially when linked together.

There is also the possibility of writing a more fitting chant or song in modern English. Well, don't immediately think of poetry, spells, Wiccans etc.. This however is not the case, though it has something to do with poetry, or rather a skill also used in poetry, designing a song has everything to with rhythm. I suggest you use metre in your chant, meaning that stressed and unstressed vowels follow each other suit. This will make the chant go rhythmically, which is exactly what you need.

95

I'm not going to get into the entire business of exactly how to write a chant, enough has been written on this subject by more skilled and qualified people. You can also use inspiring passages from the Poetic Edda or other rhythmic poetry. What you have to do is slowly and clearly sing the song of which the rhythm will bring you into trance. However, this isn't something everybody likes. For groups though, it is great as the singers tend to take you with them in their song, higher and harder, beautifully explaining the mysteries of the Gods in their lines.

In the Spirit: The Fetch, the Familiar & the Spell of the Wolf

On their way to the Sabbath the Witches would turn themselves into animals, leaving their bodies behind and travelling "in the spirit" to the Underworld. This is the origin of the stories about werewolves, women changing into hares and Witches assuming the shape of butterflies, dogs, cats etc.. In essence these are the memories of a long lost conception of the soul and the practice of the Hedgerider, as we shall see.

Werewolves, Witches & the Shape Shifters of Europe

In the trial of a freely confessed werewolf in 1692, Jürgensburg, Livonia, an eighty-year old man named Thiess, who'd never shown a lack of common sense people said, admitted that he was a werewolf. Instead of the veracious and malevolent characteristics normally attributed to werewolves, he claimed that werewolves were the 'hounds of God' and that they were the worst enemies of the Devil. On certain nights, he and other werewolves would shape shift and travel to a place 'underground' were they would fight with sorcerers for the sake of the harvest. The sorcerers stole the shoots of grain and then the werewolves would fight with the sorcerers and take the shoots back; if not, there would be famine.

A professor at the University of Riga, Witekind, once met an imprisoned werewolf. The man behaved as if mad, laughing "as if he was from a place of pleasure and not a prison." The werewolf told him he had turned into a wolf, after freeing himself from his shackles and escaping through the window, he headed for an immense river. When he asked why he had returned he replied: "I had to do it, the master wishes it"

Utrecht, Holland, in the 16th century, two sons of a motherless family confessed and accused their relatives of having the ability to change into wolves. Also they said that they had danced in the shape of cats in a certain meadow.

98

The above accounts don't picture werewolves as malevolent beings of a certain wicked character, who chase the flock in the night, nor do they seem to be 'satanic' or what have you; they appear as rather benign.

The 'Vlaamse Volksverhalen Bank', a collection of folktales collected in Belgium, contains loads of stories concerning werewolves and shape shifting black cats. One of the stories goes like this:

> *A boy who came back from the fair with his girlfriend said to her "I have to go away for a short while. If you see a huge dog approach throw your handkerchief at its mouth." The girl did as she was told. When the boy returned some hours later she saw the fibres still sticking between his teeth. The girl left the boy immediately and told everybody what had happened. At the farm where the boy worked, a jar of ointment and a collar was found, which they burned in the fire. While everything was burnin,g the boy came running and jumped into the oven and burned along with his collar.*

In this tale, you can clearly see some of the elements also found in Witchcraft. Especially the jar of ointment is an interesting parallel. Also the collar is interesting as it shows an affinity with several shape shifters in Norse Mythology, which we'll come back to later. Shockingly, these tales don't stem from a Medieval record or whatever, they were collected in 1947!

In Friuli, a region in Northern Italy, a group of Shamanic night travellers existed in the 16th and 17th century who were famous for their battles for the sake of the harvest. Sometimes theses 'good walkers' shape shifted into animals.

Also, the leader of the alleged Alpine Witch cult, Scavius, was said to be able to leave his body, though not in the shape of a wolf but in the shape of a mouse. In some periods during the Witch craze, people were afraid of Witches in the shape of cats, especially red or black cats, attacking and mortally wounding people.

The image 'Witches going to the Sabbath' is one of the earliest woodcarvings we have depicting Witches. In this woodcarving, three Witches are shown halfway through their transformation into animals. All over the testimonies and folktales, we can see the practice of the Witches, shape shifting into animals before embarking upon their journey to the Underworld.

Shape Shifting in Norse Mythology

Remarkably, shape shifting of sorcerers is also a common feature in Norse Mythology, especially associated with those skilled in the magical arts. This ability was deeply associated with the Shamanic art called Seiðr and in the fullest description of Seiðr we have, given in reference to Odin, we can see the clear affinity with the shape shifting abilities of the Hedgerider:

> "....Othin could change himself; his body then lay as if sleeping or dead, but he became a bird or wild beast, a fish or a dragon, and journeyed in the twinkling of an eye to far-off lands, on his own errands or those of other men."

Especially the words *"he then lay as if sleeping or dead"* show a connection with the Witches. They too lie as if sleeping when they fall in trance and journey to the Underworld in the shape of wolves or on the back of goats.

There are more stories about the ability of sorcerers and Seiðkona to change into animal shape and fulfil their own or somebody else's tasks. In the Saga Hjálmðérs ok Ölvérs, two foster brothers flee from a unpleasant king with magical powers. They run away with a prince who has some knowledge of magic and the king's daughter. The unpleasant king chases their ship in the form of a walrus. The prince saw the walrus and laid himself down upon the deck and told nobody to call his name; for if they did, he would die. Then they saw a 'sword-fish' swim from underneath the boat and attack the walrus. Also, the daughter goes to fight and when the walrus is finally defeated, the bodies of the prince and the daughter seem weak and tired. When wine is dripped into their mouths, they recover from their trance and weakness.

Another interesting example is found in the story of Böðvarr Bjarki in Hróls Saga Kraka in which he, Böðvarr Bjarki, goes to fight with Hjalti in the form of a bear. The fighting bear makes the armies of the enemy deal with great casualties. Finally, Hjalti misses Böðvarr and goes looking for him and finds him in his tent, sitting motionless. Böðvarr is reluctant to go with him, but when Hjalti accuses him of cowardice he gets up and says he could have been of more use to the king by remaining where he is. By then the bear had disappeared.

The above story shows strong affinities with the bersërkr and the úlfhéðnar. The bersërkr were a separate group of warriors dedicated to Odin who would burst out in a furious frenzy and kill everything in their way. Their name means 'bear-shirt' or alternatively 'bare-shirt' meaning they wore no armour in battle or bearskings over their armor. The úlfhéðnar went to battle clad in wolf skins, identifying themselves with the mighty wolf. Their dedication to Odin is characteristic to their rage, for the name Odin comes from the Old Norse 'odur' which is related to the German 'wut' which means rage, fury, but is also related to the Gothic 'wods', possessed. The continental name for Odin, Wodan, is a derivation of 'wod', meaning fury.

The superhuman power of the bersërkr and the úlfhéðnar is said to come from their magical rites in which they drank the blood of bears, thus assuming superhuman power. Certain spells were cast which made the bersërkr immune to weapons. Most frightening about their rage was that they were unbeatable. Often the heroes in the sagas took the bersërkers' lives after the rage, when their power had ceased. Their power in battle is definitely linked to their practice of becoming bear-like or wolf-like in battle, hence showing a physical form of shape shifting.

The Fetch & the Fylgia

The idea that a part of a human being may leave the body in animal shape is rooted in the idea of the fylgia. The fylgia is a personal animal 'follower' or 'double' specific to the person's character. Warriors for example, often had a strong fylgia like a wolf or bear. The fylgia was said to live in the body and could leave the body when the person was asleep – or in trance? Anyway the fylgia was thought fundamental to the continuation of life; separate from, though living in the body.

The fylgia is linked to the continental Fetch and can be attributed with the exact same qualities. Firstly, the fylgia is independent of the body and can leave it when the body is in a state of dreaming, traversing great distances – one might rightfully ask whether this is lucid dreaming. This is clearly linked to the idea of Witches leaving their bodies in the form of animals.

The idea of werewolves or man-wolves was very important in Norse society. When one was proclaimed 'warg' this person was outlawed, meaning he was no longer under the protection of the law. According to Alby Stone, the word 'warg', when spoken directly to a human, changes this person into a wolf, meaning that warg changes man into wolf. When a person was outlawed he was send out into the forest, banned from the village. Again, this relates to the symbolism of the hedge, in this case the person proclaimed warg was send into the forest, into the Underworld, thus, in a certain way, killing him.

Moreover, wolves themselves were strongly associated with the Underworld. The magical dog Gamr, was thought to be the guardian of the bridge to the Underworld. Actually, the dog that guards the Underworld is 'warg' itself.

The idea of assuming animal shape is deeply connected with the journey to the Underworld. As we've seen in the trial of Thiess, he had to change into a wolf before he could enter the Underworld, and so the man-wolf Witekind met had to change shape before he 'headed for the immense river', saying we should first assume animal shape before entering the Underworld. This trial also uses some of the ancient Germanic symbolism, for he headed for "an immense river" which refers to the infernal river so common in Norse Mythology.

The Fetch & the Battle with the Daemon

To shape shift into the Fetch before travelling to the Underworld has something to do with the conception of the soul. The soul can be seen as the 'other self' the being inside us, different yet strangely familiar. The soul is the shadow, the double, the alter-ego, the curious follower; the Fetch. This is why the animal form has to be assumed before entering the Underworld: the soul/Fetch is the unseen aspect of the human and a human cannot 'be' in the Underworld without being in this state – for humans cannot exist in the Underworld, only their soul, the Fetch.

The Fetch is that dark, frightening yet powerful aspect of us, both scaring and loving you. It protects you and at the same time it fights and tests you. This might seem strange, but battle can actually be related to in a very mystical way; the soul has to, literally, be conquered and won over. This is the battle between rational intellect and animalistic instinct, with the human as rational yet getting instinctive impulses from the Fetch. Before one can go into the Underworld one has to 'defeat', come to terms with, this dark power.

For example, I've always had this terrible fear of wolves, especially werewolves. When I was a kid, my parents would sometimes find me under the table, scared to death, because I had seen the wolf of little red riding hood on TV. Later, when I grew older, I still had this terrible fear of Werewolves, because in popular myth they have this dreadful aggressive side to them, killing everybody in their way. In the occasional nightmare, I was chased by a Werewolf and would be able to keep myself from being eaten, but not from being bitten or scratched, which would lead – according to superstition – to me turning into a Werewolf every full moon and so hurting everyone around me.

The thing I was so very afraid of was attacking other people, displaying extreme rage and the loss of control resulting in violence. Surprisingly, the wolf is my Fetch, turning 'me' into two opposites; i) my human, civilized and adapted ego and ii) my 'dark side', the raw instinctive energy of my Fetch – the same goes for you. That is actually the entire idea about the nature of the Fetch and the Persona; they are opposites and involved in a paradoxical battle – the battle between dark & light, wild & civilized, human & demon.

In the conception of the Sabbath, the Witch was given a personal animal-demon by the Devil, which was called the 'Familiar'. Often, the Witch had to feed the familiar by a hidden tooth or nipple somewhere on her body, the so called Witches' mark. They could send out the Familiar to run errands for them, but they also could ride upon the back of the Familiar to far away places.

The identification of the Familiar with a demon is quite interesting, especially since the Familiar can easily be equated to the Fetch, which leads us to an interesting place; the battle between the Witch and the Demon. The battle between the Fetch and the Witch, or the battle between the demon and the Witch is found under several guises throughout Europe.

By the penetration of Christianity in medieval society, sometimes the lore of Shamanic Battle was mingled with Christian symbolism. The adherents to the cults could not see themselves as 'evil' – which was the common opinion about Heathens – so they became

Christian, but still went to battle. This is why they thought they fought against 'Witches', because the 'Witches' were evil while they fought for the 'faith of Christ'. The idea of Witch-like Shamans fighting against the Witches caused a lot of confusion, not the least among the Shamanic warriors themselves.

The idea of battle "in the spirit" is found in the testimonies of the so called 'benandanti', the good walkers. These people, often born with a caul, would fall into a deep trance and leave their bodies, travelling to a large meadow where they would meet the malandanti, the demons and other followers of the adversary. Then they would do battle and fight for the harvest, if they lost there would be famine. According to one benandanti they went "in love of the grain".

As you might have noticed, the above account looks a lot like the trial of Thiess, the werewolf. They both went out in animal(like) shape, fought demons/Witches for the sake of the harvest and if they won the harvest would be abundant. The point is, that the benandanti lived in northern Italy while Thiess lived in Livonia – that is quite a distance.

Possibly the idea of Witches doing battle with Demons –for the sake of agriculture – was also existent in Germany somewhere at the end of the 15th and the beginning of the 16th century. In a painting by Daniel Hopfer entitled "Three Witches beating a demon on the ground". You can see a clear example of Witches fighting a demon, just like the benandanti. What's interesting about this account is that you can see a Stang lying broken on the floor, suggesting a link between the demon and the Stang. However, this would seem rather strange, as the Witches we saw in the last chapter, were the ones with a Stang. According to this painting, the Witches are 'good' and the demons 'evil' and therefore the Stang is associated with evil. So, were the Witches the enemies of the harvest?

Another painting suggests the opposite. Here a Witch is burned and the person looking happy while burning her holds a Stang and in a certain way threatens her with it, pokes up the fire. This time the evil Witch is opposed by a man (associated) with a Stang, while in the other painting the evil demon is associated with the Stang.

Here we should take a look at the Stang itself as an agricultural tool, not as a cult object. The Stang was used in the middle ages as a pitchfork and was used in the collecting of the harvest or the stacking of the gathered supplies. This would suggest an affinity between the people dependant upon the harvest, i.e. the farmer and the demon-fighting Witches.

If the above is correct, then the painter has made a mistake in associating the demon with the Stang, mingling opposite elements from the same myth. Possibly, he heard from Christian Witch hunters that the Witches carried forked pieces of wood, while a more traditional source – maybe somewhere in his youth – depicted the Witches as fighting the demons who are in turn linked to the Witches of the Inquisition. Still, the myth of Witches fighting demons shines clearly thru the confused myths.

The Witches, I think, didn't really have the idea that they fought with 'aspects of their own self', I think they wouldn't know what you're talking about! However, they did have the idea of fighting dark, gloomy forces and surely they knew about their animal fetch as part of their own soul – at least the Hedgerider did.

Maybe they were convicted for the introduction of 'new Gods' – the old Gods actually – as Socrates was convicted, partly because he talked about his daimon. And so the Witches had their own daimon, their soul with which they battled and found eternity in their victory.

Spell of the Wolf

Herodotus, a classical writer, heard rumours a about a people, called the Neuroi, who would turn into wolves every year. They would go to a river and hang their clothes on a tree and swim across the river and when they had reached the other side they would turn into wolves. Recollecting this tale, Carlo Ginzburg says in his book, 'Ecstasies':

> *"In this crossing and the attendant gestures a rite of passage has been identified: more precisely, an initiatory ceremony, or the equivalent of the infernal river that separates the world of the living from the dead."*

And that's exactly how it is. The shape shifter's journey across the river, guarded by the warg-wolf, assuming animal shape symbolises dying and being reborn again. This is the transportation of consciousness, marked by the Witching of shape, from the mind to the Fetch, the soul.

Becoming one with the Fetch marks the transformation of the human into Hedgerider, for the ego has been laid aside and the soul is known, leading up to the Underworld journey. To us, seeking to reconstruct the ways of the Hedgerider and trying to find the same experiences, a spell, a sorcerous working, to induce shape shifting is useful. The following technique is centred around the shape shift into a werewolf also known as lycanthropy, though other animals are possible too. It takes several traditional 'tools' to do it properly, these are the Stang, the ointment and the guise.

The Stang

We've already talked a lot about the Stang, we've never discussed how it can be used in ritual. As already mentioned the Stang represents the 'doorway' to the Underworld, the connecting medium by which Underworld travel is made possible. Also, it can be used as the famous pole upon which the Hedgeriders rode to the Underworld, though in ritual it can be used in an entirely different setting; here it can be used as an 'altar' and is erected as if it were the World-Tree itself. In this position, the cleft is pointed upwards symbolizing the horns of the Devil, and symbolizing the doorway as the gate to Hell. In this aspect, the Stang has become the centre of the rite, though still functioning as the World-Tree and pole of the Witches' flight.

The Stang should be erected in the middle of the space where you want to work. Where you work is actually key. Possibly you want to refrain from the living room and choose a place more suitable such as an ancient burial mound or a meadow near a large body of water. Sometimes, other physical features are thought of as important, these can include the trees and plants – the Hawthorn is considered sacred, as well as the Yew and both can be considered doors into the Underworld. Traditionally the so called 'faery rings', 'Witchrings' in Dutch, circles of mushrooms are good working places. Anyway, the place you choose should have something, a mystical yet eerie feel about it. Any place outdoors goes, for the Gods are in everything and so they are indoors – most HedgeWitches prefer outdoors though.

So before you erect the Stang, you might want to leave some offering for the elves guarding the place, especially outdoors, indoors is probably already blessed. Usually, they prefer such things like wine, milk – actually milk appears as a frequent libation in folk traditions surrounding the elves – or maybe some bread buried in the earth or suspended from a tree. You can use trees as interaction points as they function as marks of the inner landscape.

If the spirits approve – when they disapprove you'll notice – you can proceed by trusting the Stang into the ground. Then you can mark the Stang with certain symbols. Alternatively, you can mark the ground with the symbols you chose; you can use flour for this. Then you take some water and you breath the serpent's breath into it – the trance technique discussed elsewhere can be used for this. Following, you sprinkle the Stang with it, marking it holy and Otherworldly.

Some people like to light a fire in front of the Stang and I can definitely see why. Besides the significant symbolism inherent in the lightening of a fire, in the colder months of the year a fire can make the rite more comfortable. Also, fire can be used as a focus point of the rite and enhance the trance considerably.

The Ointment

If you've placed the Stang and blessed it with water, you can proceed with the following steps. You now stand or sit in front of the Stang, paying attention to the symbols carved into the Stang or marked on the floor. Take some of the flying ointment, as described under 'mugwort & wormwood' in the section on entheogens and apply it unto your wrists. This will induce trance soon enough, I suggest you pay attention to the symbols while waiting for trance to come or while practicing one of the trance techniques. If you'd rather refrain from entheogens you can use one of the trance techniques as discussed.

The ointment symbolizes the leaving behind of normal, everyday perception and makes you assume another way of perceiving. Witch-sight combined with the symbols marked on the Stang should focus you upon the purpose of the rite – lycanthropy – and the nature of the Underworld. It is important that the symbols are significant to you, not to me or anybody else, because you are the one who needs to understand them. If you are a Heathen you can use some of the runes or some of the symbols associated with Odin. Anyway, when you reach trance you should be able to picture the symbols clearly and understand where this rite will take you and not take you.

The Guise

The mask is not the magical artefact which changes you into a green faced, absurdly fluid person, but is an actual tool used to enhance shape shifting. In chapter one I quoted the Law of Vastgotaland: "*Woman, I saw you riding on a fence with loose hair and belt, <u>in the troll skin,</u> at the time when day and night are equal.*" The troll skin refers to the art of guising, wearing masks in ritual context. The mask is used to identify the Hedgerider with the Fetch and ease the way to a change of shapes.

The Guise can be used in two ways, i) as a symbol and ii) an actual shape. Basically, this means that you can either use a mask (a symbol) or the skin of an animal (the actual shape). Though the last might be preferred by some people I think it is quite difficult to find the skin of a wolf with the head of the wolf still intact so you can wear it like a wolf– not talking about what innocent bystanders will think, if they survive the acceleration of heartbeat.

Making a guise is not too difficult, you can use papier mache, but it will take great skill to produce something really beautiful. Some use wooden masks crudely cut along the shape of their face, which is then smoothed by sand paper. Next step is to paint it, preferably black, and then cover it with all sorts of feathers and other objects, sometimes runes are carved on the forehead, just above the brows.

Shape Shifting

When the Stang is installed, the ointment applied, trance invoked and the Guise put on, everything is set for the actual transformation. What will be done is the following; the Fetch as a form of the dark, instinctive, animal side of the Hedgerider is conjured to which consciousness is then transferred. This is not an easy thing to be done and I advise you to be very careful.

Lie down in front of the Stang, a few metres from it and contemplate upon the symbols once more. Then think about the fears you repressed in childhood, about the things you always wanted to do but never could, the things that scared, terrified you, but still had a weird attraction. Conjure your worst fear, face it, feel it as if it were real, drifting somewhere between you and the Stang. I know it sounds easy, but because of the trance, it will really live. You will notice some strange, dark and strong potential focussed between you and the Stang. Become it. Become that fear, realize that it *is* you and that you are there at the same time as you are here – all is one and you want to be at the place between the Stang and your body. If you are willing and Fate is on your side, you perception will change and your consciousness will be transferred to the Fetch – this means you have to *identify* with your fear and your Fetch. At the moment, you leave your body and you 'touch' the Fetch, you will change and assume the shape of the Fetch – this, to a certain extent, is death.

beyond the boundary:
the hidden Road & the
spell of the hawthorn

Now you understand the mechanisms and essence of the Underworld of Fate and the metaphysics of the worlds and your own self. You know the Witch-Goddess, you know the way of the terrible one and you are able to invoke his ecstasy, trance and leave the body in the shape of your Fetch. There is only one direction you can go now, down below. If you've truly mastered the techniques discussed and fully understand the metaphysics and Gods, you can go down into the Underworld.

The Road to Hell in Norse Mythology

However, where does the hidden road lie? That's a bit of a problem actually, for the road to elfland is indeed *hidden*. So maybe we should, again, turn to Norse Mythology to see what we can expect and how we can get there.

The most obvious of the myths is in Gylfaginning (XLIX), in which the death of Bladr is described. Baldr had dreams about himself dying and when the Gods took notice they demanded oaths from fire and water, stones, trees, birds, animals, all things not to kill Baldr. However, the treacherous Loki wasn't happy with this and went to Freyr. Disguised as an old woman, he asked him whether he had taken an oath from *all* the plants, and Freyr answered that he had not taken an oath from the mistletoe, for he deemed it too young. Loki took the mistletoe and went to Asgard. There the Gods were throwing and shooting things at Baldr, for he could not be hurt. Cunningly, Loki made one of the Gods, who was blind, shoot an arrow at Bladr made out of mistletoe and by this arrow, Baldr was killed.

The Gods could not rest and grieve and they asked whether one of them had the courage to ride to Hell and Fetch Baldr. The man who stepped forth went by the name Hermódr and was one of the sons of Odin and also Baldrs brother. He took Odin's steed, Sleipnir and set on his way:

"Now this is to be told concerning Hermódr, that he rode nine nights through dark dales and deep, so that he saw not before he was come to the river Gjöll and rode onto the Gjöll-Bridge; which bridge is thatched with glittering gold. Módgudr is the maiden called who guards the bridge; she asked him his name and race, saying that the day before there had ridden over the bridge five companies of dead men; but the bridge thunders no less under thee alone, and thou hast not the color of dead men. Why ridest thou hither on Hel-way?' He answered: 'I am appointed to ride to Hel to seek out Baldr. Hast thou perchance seen Baldr on Hel-way?' She said that Baldr had ridden there over Gjöll's Bridge,--'but down and north lieth Hel-way.'

'Then Hermódr rode on till he came to Hel-gate; he dismounted from his steed and made his girths fast, mounted and pricked him with his spurs; and the steed leaped so hard over the gate that he came nowise near to it. Then Hermódr rode home to the hall and dismounted from his steed, went into the hall, and saw sitting there in the high-seat Baldr, his brother; and Hermódr tarried there overnight.....'

In this myth, you can clearly see the elements of the journey into the Underworld. Hermódr takes the magical steed of Odin, Sleipnir and he rides nine nights and days, which is a symbolic period, often signifying some sort of initiation or other highly symbolic quantity.

Then he comes to the Hell-river, the infernal body of water separating the land of the living from the land of the dead. Here it is called "gjöll", and is one of the rivers springing from Hvergilmir, the Seething cauldron suited in Niflheim. Also, it is said to have knives flowing in it and is freezing cold.

Then he goes on to cross the bridge, which is "glittering gold", making more noise than five companies of men. He rides until he reached Hell – only then dismounting his steed. *"but down and north lieth Hel-way"* is the most interesting passage as it points at a direction considered synonymous with the Underworld, the north – note that all the wells, of wisdom, Wyrd and water, are suited in the north. Actually, the north and the below can be considered one and the same, because 'north' comes from the a word bearing connotations with 'down below'.

After that, the traveller has to use the magical powers of the steed to leap over the gate of Hell, or else he could not enter. This suggests that the journey isn't easy and that it takes some sort of 'test' to be able to enter the Underworld.

Another story of the journey to the Underworld is found in 'Baldrs Draumar' in which Baldr has unpleasant dreams and Odin goes to the Underworld to seek a deceased Volva who can interpret Baldrs Dream.

> *" Then Othin rose, | the enchanter old,*
> *And the saddle he laid | on Sleipnir's back;*
> *Thence rode he down | to Niflheim deep,*
> *And the hound he met | that came from Hell."*

> *"Bloody he was | on his breast before,*
> *At the father of magic | he howled from afar,*
> *Forward rode Othin, | the earth resounded*
> *Till the house so high | of Hel he reached."*

In these few lines, the journey of Odin to the realm of Hell is described. In the second line you can again see the use of the magical steed Sleipnir, who can be considered the same as the World-Tree, for both are the "steed of the Terrible One". Riding on his steed, he went to Niflheim and met a hound "that came from Hell" meaning he met the warg-hound at the gate of Hel. This being was sometimes called Garmr according to Völúspá. It is really important, as this warg-hound reflects the reversal and aura of death surrounding the realm of Hell. The wolfish energy of this being denotes the change of life into death, order into chaos and, naturally, of man into animal and human into Fetch. After the growls of the warg-hound, *"house so high | of Hell he reached"*, plainly meaning he had reached the Underworld.

Another legend about the Underworld is found in the story of Hadingus, already discussed in Chapter Two. The hero, Hadingus, is taken down into the earth, to the realm of the nether Gods, by an old woman. First, they have to go through mist and darkness and then along a road; through a sunny land where plants grow. They have to pass a river, which contains all sorts of weapons, then they cross by a bridge. She takes him to a high wall over which she throws a dead cock, which makes sounds as if alive again when having reached the other side.

In this story, there are some traditional elements, only more confused this time. There is the journey through mist and darkness and then over the river. This river bears resemblance to Gjöll, it too has weapons flowing in it and also a bridge spans across it. And, of course, there is the wall which cannot be passed by the living – only by magic or a magical steed.

From the above, I think we can most clearly conclude that the traveller has to take the Terrible One's Steed and travel over dark things and misty waters; then across the Gjöl by passing the golden bridge, meanwhile meeting the Underworld guardian, Garmr. However, the journey is not free from perils as testified by the Spell of Gróa, see the appendix, which she spoke to her son embarking upon the journey along the road to Hell.

As testified by this spell, the road to Hell is full of dangers; enemies behind your back; possibility to wander lost of your way; waters that will make you lose your way; many enemies on the road to Hell; inability to walk forward; waves and winds so hard that boats shall not prevail; extreme cold gripping your heart; the curse of Christian women; giants testing your wisdom. All these are found on the hidden road to Elf-Land and it is not without passing the Giant's Test that you will be allowed into the Underworld.

Actually the ninth stanza of the spell is key in the perception of the hidden road. *"and thy mouth of words full wise"* means you will have to speak truth to the giant testing you. Possibly, the giant you meet will ask you some ridiculous question or riddle, the answer though has nothing to do with human "wit" or "intelligence". It has to do with speaking the truth of things, speaking in the irrational logic of the Underworld and its inhabitants. You have to prove you're worthy of the name "Hedge-Rider", by speaking the Otherworldly language. So when you embark on your journey and some being asks you something, answer him/her in truth, not in logic, but in the words springing from your mind, immediately, without thinking about it.

The Hedgerider's Hidden Road to Elf-Land

The conception of the Underworld in Norse Mythology and in the mind of the Witches was sometimes strikingly similar, though, do the two coincide when it comes to the road to the Underworld?
Throughout this book I've presented several testimonies and trials in which the lore of the Hedgerider was clearly demonstrated. In the testimony of Thiess and the talk between Witekind and a werewolf show some distinct, Germanic features. Indeed the name for the Underworld, Thiess, used is the same, Hell. Also, the idea of the infernal river separating the realms. Witekind's werewolf headed for "an immense river", suggesting a link with the river Gjöll of Norse Mythology. First, Thiess said he went across the sea, correcting himself later saying he went underground. Maybe these two are the same? Crossing the river and then going underground or the other way around.

In a Witch trial in Val di Fiemme, a man said he went to the good game of Diana. First he went to a lake where he met a man who himself was black and cloaked in black, who made him renounce

Christianity. Then he was allowed to pass over the lake into the mountain.

Also interesting is the lore of the black dog in relation to the Witches. The black dog appears in the Witch-trials as the Devil or the Witch's familiar. At Brecy in 1616 he appeared as a black dog talking and standing straight up.

Then there is the notorious doctor Faust, who was said to have a black poodle called Mephistopheles. This black shaggy dog was, in fact, the Devil assuming the shape of the Witch's familiar.

In 'Teutonic Mythology' Grimm states that several names of the Devil come from words meaning wolf. Possibly the God of the dead took the shape of a Hellhound or wolf as he was in itself the terror of death, as well the inflictor of this terror, the warg-hound. This would give an entirely new meaning to the idea of the Devil appearing as a black dog to the Witches. Though the Witch hunters probably changed the entire testimonies, or the Witches only said that was expected of them, the black dog still has, definite Hellish symbolism attached to its appearance. In this respect, when the Witch met the black dog, she met the Underworld guardian who, in his newly found Devil-form, initiated the Underworld experience in her and so inflicted the journey to the Sabbath.

In the medieval and renaissance journey to the Sabbath, there are some parallels with the journey to the Underworld in Norse Mythology. Obviously, the ride on the 'Stang', the wooden pole, shows some parallel characteristics; the fashion in which it is ridden, like a steed and both the steed of the Terrible One and the Stang are made of wood.

The elements found in the Norse conception appear parallel to the Witches. First, there is the use of a wooden steed; then there is the warg-hound and the black dog; and the "immense river", Gjöll. Though in the Witch trials, the elements appear confused and mingled, often in a different order, they probably once were part of a more coherent, complex mythological body which was part of the Hedgeriders' beliefs.

The Gate to Hell

The above is really useful, as it gives us the opportunity to explain more things about the Witches and the nature of the beliefs of the Hedgerider. However, to the practitioner, it doesn't give a clue as to where and how to engage in contact with the Underworld. Obviously taking a horse – a magical horse actually – and riding over dark valleys won't do the trick. There must be found some connection between *physical reality* and *inner reality*, leading up to a physical connection where the inner and outer are connected in such a way that the inner can be accessed. But, where to find such a place? Definitely not in the myths of Norse Mythology we've already taken a look at, this time we'll have to do with the folklore from the continent.

Firstly we can turn to the passage of the Homilies of Aelfric:
> "Yet fares Witches to where roads meet, and to Heathen burials
> with their phantom craft and call to them the Devil, and he comes
> to them in the dead man's likeness, as if he from death arises, but
> she cannot cause that to happen, the dead to arise through her
> wizardry."

In this passage it is clearly said that Witches go to Heathen burials and the crossroads. In Norse Mythology, burial mounds appear as entrances to the world below. Mostly, it rather gives access to the realm of the inhabitant than the Underworld itself. Some sorcerers can, however, enter these mounds and access the inner parts of the Underworld. Possibly, the burial mounds were centres of Underworld-contact.

Also, the places "where roads meet" can be considered one of the contact points of the Hedgerider. The crossroads were considered sacred to the Classical Greek Goddess Hecate, who was also the Goddess of the Underworld. Though possibly the idea of the crossroads being a place of the dead can be linked to the positioning of the gallows on these places so the hanged, and angered, dead could not find their way to the houses of the living. The Gallows are sacred to Odin, one of the Devil's forebears, and so the crossroads can be sacred to him as well. In essence, the Gallow-places from which the gallow-ways depart are one and the same as the crossroad and are drenched with the spirit of Hell and death. So, here too can contact with the Underworld be sought.

More hints at those special places can be found in folklore and stories. The most peculiar one is the idea of a place being haunted. Many houses, and especially grave yards, are considered 'haunted' at the special 'in-between times' when the boundary is thinner and the dead can roam the earth freely. If the spirits of the dead can enter this world, then the living should be able to enter the Otherworld. Although in Christian times, death was considered an 'evil'. To the Heathens, it was more benign, more like a mother calling her children to rest – in fact, the Heathen Gods take care of their children, unlike the Judeo-Christian God. So, if the spirits of the dead came back, it was because the boundary between the worlds was thin and practically non-existent.

So, if you look for a place to go down below, listen to the old spinsters and their stories about 'haunted places' or 'ghosts', maybe even common myths about Witches assembling in certain places. Check the history of the town you live in, for certain there will be some ancient local superstition about a haunted mansion or Witches' gathering. You can also search for long-forgotten tracks along which the dead were transported to the graveyard. On these roads, the Wild Hunt is said to pass and are 'thin' too. Or simply go to a place where everything is 'wild' and scares you. Often these places are 'haunted' as well. It is in these places that you can make a bond. Make an offering to the guardians of that place and use trees and stones to interact with them.

Another possibility, well documented, is the use of certain trees. One of the plants renowned for its elf-energy is the hawthorn. Several folk stories tell us about how people fell asleep under a hawthorn and were then taken by the elves to their underground realm. In fact, the Old English word for Hedgerider, 'haegetesse' is intimately connected with the hawthorn. The 'haeg' refers to 'Haga' which can mean hedge and more specifically hawthorn. The hawthorn, in this sense, is in such a way connected with Hedgecraft, that the plant can be considered central to the Hedgeriders and is therefore one of the most powerful ways to engage in Otherworldly contact.

The Spell of the Hawthorn

Now I'm going to provide you with a sorcerous working; a 'spell', by which you can enter the Underworld. I advise you to be really careful and cautious for these things aren't to be toyed with.

As the name already states, this Spell is all about the Hawthorn which is used as an entrance point into the Underworld. Secondly, it relies heavily upon your personal bond with your animal-fetch or certain ancestral guardians – without the contact of spirits, this rite is impossible. Thirdly, it relies upon the active participation of the mind in the concepts and symbols described in this book – if you don't believe what's in this book, or any other *good* book about, Seiðr, Traditional Witchcraft or Germanic Shamanism don't bother to try.

The things necessary for this rite are, as usual, the ointment, the Stang and the guise. Also, certain wooden stakes, 'rune-sticks' are utilized, along with the tools used to mark the signs on the floor and such.

The Hawthorn

To begin this rite you'll have to find a good hawthorn, fairly big and with healthy roots and leaves. They have the tendency to let their outer branches hang lower than the branches at the trunk, meaning you get sort of a huge bowl turned upside down. This you'll need, and so you'll have to find a fairly old hawthorn.

To some people it can be a real pain in the ass to locate a good hawthorn. Point is, they don't grow everywhere. In the region where I live they are used as hedges to separate the parishes of the farmers and as natural fences to keep the flocks in and so are fairly common. Because some areas used for agriculture haven't been used as extensively, hawthorns have gotten the chance to grow huge and old. If you really can't find a hawthorn I suggest you look for some other entrance equally powerful.

You begin by pouring a libation of milk in front of the hawthorn, asking the spirits of the hawthorn – i.e. the elves – and the spirits of the place to aid you in your working, but also in the journey to the Underworld. Say thanks.

Then initiate the prayers to the old Gods, ask Fate to be with you and the black one to aid you in your journey. It doesn't have to be complicated or highly poetic, just talk to them and ask them for their help. If you truly give yourself to them, they will not ignore your prayers.

Then, approach the hawthorn. Take a willow branch and break it into three even parts about 20 cm long and mark each of them with the runes you find significant. Personally, I prefer to mark the names of the old Gods upon these stakes. In my native language they go like this: "Vrouw Holle" or "Vrouw Vreke" & "Wodan". In English they are "Dame Holda" or "Lady Freya" & "Woden". Maybe a word signifying the presence of your Fetch can be used also. Stick the stakes into the ground so that they form a triangle with the trunk of the hawthorn in the middle.

Some Witches like to draw the lines between the stakes in flour on the ground; others prefer to link the three by a circle. Personally, I prefer the circle, as it represents a snake biting its own tail, everlasting Fate or the Underworld initiation itself. It is up to you.

The Stang

> *"By the old Gods, Wodan, Allfather. Dark Master of the Wild Heir, Master of the Black Door. Holda, Lady of the Hills, Queen of the Elves and Mistress of the Cold River. Both do I ask to help me, be present and aid me in this working."*

This can be how you begin praying once you've set yourself against the trunk. You have to repeat praying like this endlessly, finally ending with the clear-cut intention to enter the Underworld.

Then, take the Stang and anoint it with the Witches' oil described under 'mugwort' in the section on entheogens. This is a highly symbolic gesture, and should be combined with the awakening of trance. Next, the Stang is placed on the ground, with the cleft to the South, as if it departs to the North. If you're lucky, this matches the exact length between the trunk and the Northern perimeter of the circle. If it's too short, you have a problem, too long isn't a problem at all. Sit against the trunk with your face to the North, so that you're lined up with the Stang.

The Guise

Now you should have something you associate with your Fetch, possibly this is the guise. You have to put it on your face. If it is a word you can write it twice into the ground, left and right of the Stang. Vowels can be chanted and visions can be visualized.

This is a very important part in the working as it is alldependant on the summoning of the animal-fetch. Close your eyes. If you've done the Spell of the Wolf several times, you should be having some sort of bond with your Fetch, now you can utilize that bond to summon it to the surface of your consciousness. It doesn't matter how you do it. There are no rules in the realm of Witchery, everything is permitted.

Once your Fetch appears, you have to merge with it. Not like you're used to, as in the Spell of the Wolf. You have to let it in, while not getting out of your body. There is only one way to do this; you have to let it in by breathing in strongly, preferably you can use the technique of Serpent Swaying to do this. You have your entire breath focussed upon letting the Fetch in. Inhale its consciousness and feel its animal energy rush through your body. Once you've merged, you can sit for a couple of minutes, waiting to proceed with the actual technique.

Walking the Hidden Road

The rest of this Spell is left fully up to Fate and can only work if She permits. With your senses, start focussing upon the hawthorn behind you. Can you smell it? Hear its leaves rustling in the wind? Can you feel your back against the smooth bark? Hold that feeling. Feel your back against the trunk. At once, the trunk opens! One moment you can feel the bark. The next moment, you can feel the trunk burst open, letting you fall down. You tumble and tumble and can only see the darkness around you. And then......yes, then it's all up to the Queen.

It should be noted that some people still have awareness in their bodies while journeying to the Underworld, having the eerie feeling of being in two places at once. This means some people can feel the bark burst open, while at the same time feeling the bark not bursting open! There are also alternative scenarios. Maybe you see a gate or a burial mound in a trance-vision and you can approach it, maybe the elves come and take you to their Queen. It is all possible. Trance-vision is, however, one of the most likely scenarios, meaning you see things in your minds eye.

The Sacred Marriage:
The Fetch & the Quest
for the Underworld
Bride

We've almost covered the entire subject of the Underworld and so this book is coming to an end. You already know how to change your perception by using trance techniques, how you can leave your body and how you induce Otherworldly journeys. This means, in essence, you've dissected your mind, found the secrets of the soul and are only a few inches away from the completion of what is called the Underworld initiation.

The Bride in the Deep Below

Though we've covered the quest for wisdom and what lore is attached to it, there is another more illogical and irrational goal to be found in the Underworld; this is the quest for a unknown (elf-) woman. In the myth, the warrior falls madly in love with some unknown lady of impeccable beauty who he has to search and find – in the Underworld. I know this sounds like the typical Celtic plot, however, examples are also found in Norse Mythology sometimes mentioning the power of Love and the journey to Hell more explicitly than the Celtic variations.

In the Saga of Svipdag, Svipdagsmál, a story is told of a young man who has fallen in love with a supernatural maiden, Menglöð, who, unluckily, lives in the Underworld. However, his love is so great, his longing so painful, that he has to seek her in the Underworld. First, he goes to his mother's mound, asking her to chant mighty charms so that he will not be hurt on the way below – we've already discussed these charms in Chapter 7 and they are fully printed in the Appendix. Then he goes down to the Underworld, where he meets a giant to whom he gives a false name and asks questions about the Fate of the Gods, but also about Menglöð and whether she has a man lying in her arms. The giant replies she does not, for Svipdag, the young man who went out on the quest, is Fated to be with her. Then Svipdag reveals his true nature and then they live 'happily ever after':

"Alike we yearned; | I longed for thee,
And thou for my love hast longed;
But now henceforth | together we know
Our lives to the end we shall live."

Another example is found in Skírnísmal. Freyr sees a beautiful maiden in Jotunheim, the realm of the giants, and gets such a longing for her that he becomes filled with feelings of despair and misery. One of his servants, Skirnir, says he will go and bring the maiden back to him — it is likely that Skirnir is a aspect of Freyr. Skirnir takes Freyr's magical sword which fights for itself, which will leave him without arms in the final battle, and takes Freyr's (?) magical steed. He passes into Jotunheim and enters through a gate in the fence to which fierce dogs were bound — this clearly resembles some of the symbolism attached to the Underworld we've already encountered, suggesting that she did not live in Jotunheim, but in Hell. When Skirnir asks a giant how he can pass the dogs the giant replies:

Art thou doomed to die | or already dead,
Thou horseman that ridest hither?

Actually, asking whether he is dead and thus having the right to pass, or doomed to die — i.e. never to return from the realm he is about to enter. (my note…incomplete sentence?) Then Skirnir goes to the maiden fancied by Freyr, however, she is reluctant to come with him. He threatens her with all sorts of miseries — actually threatening her to die a second death; meaning she will never return from the deep void of Niflheim. Then the maiden comes with him and she sets off to meet Freyr in some forest.

Supernatural Lovers in Witchery

The idea of a lover from the Underworld was quite common during the Witch-trials and was part of the standard conception of the image of the Witch. The Witch was said to have an 'incubus', a demonic spirit who would have intercourse with the Witch while sleeping. Often, this would manifest itself in erotic dreams resulting in orgasm. To the clergy, this was a very 'evil' deed, for the Witch enjoyed sexual freedom and for women this, according to Christian doctrine, is indeed sinful.

The idea of incubi and succubae – these were female spirits visiting the male populace – was also used as 'excuse-demon' explaining all sorts of, human, crimes such as sexual abuse and rape – often used as comforting explanation for rape by family members and other people enjoying the trust and confidence of the victim.

In the trial of Dame Alice Kyteler, a woman from Anglo-Norman decent, in the beginning of the 14th century was one of the first to take place in Ireland. Her earlier three husbands died while married to her and when she disinherited the stepchildren of her fourth husband – who was also mysteriously ill – she was accused of Witchcraft. She had a familiar in the shape of a black shaggy dog, called Robin Artisson or Robin Son of Art and he was also mentioned as incubus.

The idea of incubi and succubae is, I think, mostly connected with the Christians imagining things, blaming it on 'the Devil' rather than there were actually demons trying to have sex with monks or "good Christian women" – can't see why you would choose a monk or a "good Christian woman" if you could pick *everybody*. However, some lore may be attached to it. As said, the person would be asleep when the demon would visit. Normally this wouldn't seem significant, but in the case this is *really important* because maybe the Witch wasn't asleep but had fallen into trance while visiting the Underworld, thus turning her dreams into an Otherworldly experience.

 This changes the entire idea of the 'demonic' nature of the incubi and succubae. In this respect, the incubi & succubae hold the same powers as the brides of Norse Mythology, in the sense that they are

130

sought after in trance, in the Underworld and are married to the seeker, merge with the seeker.

The Sacred Marriage in Hedge Witchery

So, Hedgeriders would embark upon their journey into the below, dying and being resurrected again to find a supernatural bride – what does this bride mean? The bride is the counterpart of the human persona, a manifestation of the Fetch. To a man, she is a woman and to a woman he is a man. She represents the anima, the female side of the man's soul. Instead of focusing upon the order-chaos polarity of the human-animal and so seeing them as conflicting, as something to be conquered, the fetch-lover is focussed upon the *merging* of opposites.

The merging of opposites is also known under the Latin name, Hiëros Gamos, the Sacred Marriage. That is what we're dealing with here: the marriage in the sacred dimension of the self. This has been a theme throughout mythological history, often reflected in the marriage between a God and a Goddess as a final solution.
The Hedgerider seeks the Fetch, the soul, inside the Underworld and while doing this, the HedgeWitch dies, the persona fades – the Odinic death & rebirth – then the new mind has to battle the soul – the battle between Witches and demons – and conquer the dark aspects of the self. In the last stance, the HedgeWitch has to merge with the soul to fully complete the Underworld initiation. That's what the Hiëros Gamos is about, the merging with the soul.

The representation of the Fetch as bride/husband is really important. Copulation is, in spiritual sense respectively, the full act of merging with the other half and one becomes truly One with the Other. When the Fetch is represented as the other half, it is the soul, found and conquered, willing to merge with the human half. Indeed, they are opposites, the objective and subjective, the dark and Light, unknown and known, woman and man, man and woman, and

131

when they merge, the soul is truly found, truly awakened and the consciousness truly shifted.

It goes even deeper than this. As we've discussed, the doctrine of Wyrd in relation to Godhead and the immortal soul and the prone mind the sacred marriage with the fetch-lover becomes even more meaningful. The fetch-lover can be seen as the deeper layers of Fate, the strand of the soul, and when one merges with these the more superficial layers are killed off and one now only acts from the basis of truth, no longer subject to the former conditions of culture and socialisation – this the state a truly wise person has reached. Now, the Underworld initiation is truly complete and the Hedgeriders can act on their own, seeking only to do the wise thing, having fully mastered wisdom. The soul and the mind are One.

Musings from the hearth: living & Initiating the Old Ways

This book is almost coming to its close and so a conclusion should be drawn – for if there is no conclusion, there is no point in all of this being written. In conclusion one can ask: "what have I learned?"

There are many different things that can be learned from this book, only, the one question we set out to answer is fully answered: "what it Witchcraft?" I think that Witchcraft is Shamanic, meaning it is centred around the contact with, arousal of and journey to the Underworld. This entire work has been centred on this one doctrine, Shamanism, and so I hope to have fully shown you the depths and creepy corners of the Witches' Underworld and the beliefs surrounding this place.

A link has been established between the mythology of the Norse and the surviving beliefs of the Witches, the lore shows to be intimately connected, resulting in the idea that the Witches, the Hedgeriders, *were* actually Teutonic and in the large picture, Germanic.

We've covered the symbolism of the Hedge and so the meaning and duty of the Hedgeriders. We have delved into the Underworld, both from Norse Mythology and medieval folklore, only to emerge to find that the Underworld is rooted in a fatalist conception of the world and its events – Fate – and deeply linked with the Goddess of the Witches. Then, we discussed the cheating of Fate and the purpose of death & rebirth and how it is related to the journey and the Allfather of Norse and Germanic Mythology. Following, we dug into the realms of extra-sensory reality and the magical wooden steeds – also known as the Witches' Broom – and how ecstasy or trance can be achieved. Then we immerged in a full discussion of shape shifting, how to achieve it and the conception of the soul and the Fetch and how they are related to the daemonic battle. Next was the discussion of the hidden road, a map to guide you to the Underworld and how the journey can be undertaken, resulting in the Spell of the Hawthorn. The last chapter was a short one, discussing the lore surrounding the Sacred Marriage and how the

Witch eventually merges with the self and by this freeing herself from the bonds of Fate; ultimately leading to wisdom.

Living the Old Ways

The essential question of this all is not to find the knowledge, that's not too difficult, but *how* to relate to the beliefs of the Old Ways. There's no easy way of doing this, I think. There needs to be a fundamental change in world-view, a deep knowledge that everything is as it is, resulting in the idea that the Gods are here, that they speak to you in the world around you, that Fate exists and the Underworld is real, more real than the wind against your cheek, more visible than the house you live in, more loud than the scream of a newborn baby. It is these things that should be awakened.

I think there is one way to do this, and that is to listen to the inner and see the outer as a manifestation of the inner. This means to let your inner voice speak. Your inner feelings, the stirring of your Fetch, can be used to determine what is happening outside. Ultimately, the inner can be seen as that which shapes the outer, or vice versa, of course. In essence, these two aren't separate and influence each other more than you might think. In the events of nature, Fate ultimately shows Her will. Contemplating upon these things, in telling the Fate of life by the omens of nature, there is the real possibility of awakening the world-view of the Heathen.

Also, simply praying to the Gods, relating to them in a very personal way, can aid the change of world-view. Mention them when you curse. Try to ban the words "Christ", "Jesus" etc.. and replace them by words more proper to a follower of the Old Ways – or just don't curse at all.

Something very important in Heathenry, and thus Hedge Witchery, is the bringing of sacrifice. Sacrificing to the Gods is one of those things that will bring you into close contact with them. The following is, in Heathenry, called the "symbol": just take a cup and fill it with wine or mead and hold it up to the sky, preferably at some sacred site, and ask the Gods to be with you, to bless you. Simply dedicate the offering to them and pour it onto the ground.

Also, more valuable or symbolic things may be offered to them. An interesting example of this is found in the Witches' "Houzle", which plainly means 'sacrifice'. In this rite, a bowl of wine and a plate of bread are blessed in the name of "the Lady and the Lord of Dread". Then the wine is poured upon the bread, which is then used to anoint the participants "in the name of the Old People". The rest of it is offered in the same fashion as in the symbol.

The essence of this rite is becoming one with the Ancestral Current. Because the participants are anointed in the name of the Old People, who are the ancestors, their consciousness takes part in the Ancestral Current, which is the sum of all the lore, knowledge and praxis concerning the specific tradition – meaning that the ancestral knowledge is transferred to the participant.

The concept of ancestral knowledge, ancestral gnosis or ancestral memories is intimately tied up with traditional Witchcraft and gives a completely new 'freshness' to Hedge Witchery. What it basically comes down to is this: the ancestors are the people who've gone before us. They guard the sacred knowledge and communicate it to those who can show they're genuine. They are the guardians of the Witch-traditions and initiate a new tradition as they see fit, this means a (hedge) Witch always has a tradition to which he or she belongs, only sometimes this person isn't taught in the flesh, but in the spirit, by spirits.

The above may sound ridiculous; however, the ancestors *do* exist and are definitely part of the inner. They are the initiators of sudden insights into lore and sometimes provide new lore. They can show you the deepest secrets of Hedge Witchery and can aid you on the Hedgepath.

The idea of the ancestral memories and the ancestors should be central within your workings, for it is these two things that will keep your praxis and faith alive and changing, evolving as it were. Every time you do a houzle, a symbol or any other working, try to dedicate some to the ancestors.

Induction into the Witching Way

This brings us to a set of practices not much talked about in public – in private, well, I can't know that for sure. Namely, the dedication to the old Gods & the Ancestors. In modern Wiccan literature, there is much talk of 'self-initiation' and 'dedication', but that isn't quite the same as we're talking about here. The True initiation isn't self-inflicted and is way more complex than a simple rite of stating one's intentions – as you've seen, the Underworld initiation covers way more than that. However, there is a rite that can be considered an initiation in which the candidate binds him- or herself to the Gods & the Ancestors. This is the acknowledging of the 'hidden family', by which the Witch confirms his or her (Ancestral) line and in which the Witch 'binds' the Gods to her – meaning the Witch is acknowledged by the Gods as 'genuine' and almost considered 'family'.

Of course, this isn't a simple rite and isn't something to be done lightly, as from this point there is no going back. You engage in a two way pact with the Gods which cannot be broken, by either side. There is no standard way of going about this and every Witch probably has her/his own version of the initiation, or Induction rather. Standard is always a fire kindled to represent the ancestral fires, some sort of 'oath' sworn to the Gods and a two-way blood sacrifice, by which the Gods & Ancestors and the HedgeWitch are bound together.

Always begin a working with an offering to the spirits of the place and ask their blessing. Now, I'm going to give you an example of the oath, and I advise you to delete and add things as you see fit, though the essence should remain the same:

By the words of the Old Gods,
Dame Holle, Mistress of the midnight skies,
Queen of the Elf-Hill and the Well of Hell
Master of the Hidden Craft, Witchfather,
Black Lord of Dread and Holy Fear,
Both of you do I beg to be here,
And bless my Fire, and kindle the Sacred Fire within my heart.

The fire is lit.

Here do I --, son/daughter of [name father] & [name mother]
stand before you,
With my hart in my hand, the Stang in the other,
Before the Black God and the Elf-Queen do I bring my sacrifice,
My Fate and hart in your hands, my will fully given,
Here do I stand, with my intentions clear,
And I bring a Stang & Skull, and hold them in my left hand,
Witchmaster and Queen of elves, with this do I swear allegiance
to you,
Here my sacrifice is brought, with the ancestors as my witness,
Do I testify that I will always hold your honour high,
And I will always carry you in my heart,

The sacrifice is brought and poured upon the Stang. The left-hand is symbolic of your Otherworldly side. Movements and holding of objects is always done with the left-hand or left-way to signify the Otherworldly intentions of the Hedgerider.

To the Elf-Folk of the Venus-Mountain,
My great, great forebears, Ancestors,
Here do I acknowledge you and ask you to do the same for me,
For we are bound by blood and soul.

138

I want to stress again that this isn't something you do lightly; there is no going back from here. Now let's talk about the consequences of the above. First of all, you can count upon the Ancestors to acknowledge you as one of their kin, which can be very useful when you try to reconstruct an entire system of Witchery, including rituals and such. Secondly, the Gods are now engaged in a two-way pact, so when you bring an offering to them, they should repay you with something of the same value. I know this sounds really 'impersonal' but is not, for it aids your bond with the deity. This means the houzle/symbol can also be described as 'magic', a supernatural way of achieving your wishes.

After this petition, the houzle/symbol should be performed every full moon and preferably also on those days that are called the 'Ember Days' and the Zwölften. These are: first of February, also known as Maria Light Mass, First of May which is called Walpurgisnight, first of August commonly known as Bread Mass and first of November, remembered as All Hallows or Halloween, as well as the period between Christmas and the arrival of the three wise kings. Study the symbolism of these, Christianized, feasts and honour the Gods & Ancestors on those days and, possibly, perform the Spell of the Wolf or the Spell of the Hawthorn on those days, so that you may enter into the sacred times and enjoy the company of the Gods.

appendix

Appendix I: Gallery of Witches

These paintings stem from the late medieval and early renaissance period and show the conception of the Witch in those days. These are here printed because I believe them to provide essential information about the Witches. The paintings give a rough example of the Pagan lore still embedded in the archetype of the Witch and I advise you to locate these in the paintings. There the obvious elements of Stang and flying ointment, but also a rite resembling the houzle is depicted, as well as horse and human skulls.

Hans Baldung Grien - Hexen beim Schadenszauber

Hans Frank Meister – Witches

Germany, 1485 – 1522

Geiler von Keisersberg – Witches

Germany, 1516

Witches' Flight – J. Otmar

1489

Hexen Meysterey
Germany – 1545

Reinard Lutz – Warhafftige Zeitung von den gottlosen Hexen

Schletstatt, Germany – 1571

Appendix II: Spells of Gróa

"Then first I will chant thee | the charm oft-tried,
That Rani taught to Rind;
From the shoulder whate'er | mislikes thee shake,
For helper thyself shalt thou have.

"Then next I will chant thee, | if needs thou must travel,
And wander a purposeless way:
The bolts of Urth | shall on every side
Be thy guards on the road thou goest.

"Then third I will chant thee, | if threatening streams
The danger of death shall bring:
Yet to Hel shall turn | both Horn and Ruth,
And before thee the waters shall fail.

"Then fourth I will chant thee, | if come thy foes
On the gallows-way against thee:
Into thine hands | shall their hearts be given,
And peace shall the warriors wish.

"Then fifth I will chant thee, | if fetters perchance
Shall bind thy bending limbs:
O'er thy thighs do I chant | a loosening-charm,
And the lock is burst from the limbs,
And the fetters fall from the feet.

"Then sixth I will chant thee, | if storms on the sea
Have might unknown to man:
Yet never shall wind | or wave do harm,
And calm is the course of thy boat.

"Then seventh I chant thee, | if frost shall seek

149

To kill thee on lofty crags:
The fatal cold | shall not grip thy flesh,
And whole thy body shall be.

"Then eighth will I chant thee, | if ever by night
Thou shalt wander on murky ways:
Yet never the curse | of a Christian woman
From the dead shall do thee harm.

"Then ninth will I chant thee, | if needs thou must strive
With a warlike giant in words:
Thy heart good store | of wit shall have,
And thy mouth of words full wise.

Appendix III: Vocabulary

numbers

1734
This number was used by the Traditional Witch Robert Cochrane do describe the Witch-Goddess. The numbers 1-7-3-4 describe several aspects of the Goddess.
See   1734-Tradition
          Traditional Witchcraft

1734-Tradition
The tradition – headed by Joe Wilson – brought to America by the writings and letters of Robert Cochrane. In several letters he encoded hints which are unravelled by the followers. However, in the later days they are often considered the 'fraud-squad' because they mingled their practice with Gardnerian Wicca and often revolved around High or Ceremonial Magic rather than real Witchcraft.
See   1734
          Traditional Witchcraft

a

Amunita Muscaria
Fly Agaric (Amunita Muscaria) is the traditional red with white spots capped mushroom. It has some usage in Siberian Shamanic practices and is also associated with the faery in the British Isles
See   Entheogen

Arthame
A black hilted knife mentioned in the Key of Salomon, Claviculis

Salamonis. It is especially used in ritual to force the spirits. It was adapted by Gardner and he changed the spelling into 'athame' for his new religion.

See   Athame

Athame
A black hilted knife used by British Traditional Wiccans, also many New-Age Wiccans use the athame. It is specifically used by the Wiccans to cast the circle, deal with any magical working and the blessing of certain liquids and objects. It originally appeared in the Key of Salomon, as the 'arthame'. Belief states the athame may never be used to cut anything, especially living organisms.

See   Arthame

Artimesia Absinthium
Also known as 'common wormwood' or just wormwood. it contains the chemical component 'thujon' and is the major ingredient in the infamous drink absinth. Thujone produces a clear state of mind and the herb itself is considered sacred to Artemis and the moon. Also known for its extremely bitter taste.

See   Artimesia Vulgaris
        Entheogen

Artimesia Vulgaris
Also known as mugwort, also contains high levels of thujone and is also sacred to the moon and Artemis. Also known as St. Johns-plant – not wort! – and is used in several folk customs surrounding midsummer.

See   Artimesia Absinthium
        Entheogen

Asatru

This is a name used to denote the ancient beliefs of the Northern Peoples by modern reconstructionist. The word literally means 'loyal to the Aesir'. They try to reconstruct the way of the ancient Norse and Germanic People by taking a close look at the Edda's and other Saga's handed down. The ethics are centred around the Nine Noble Virtues. Their cosmology upholds the nine worlds, Wyrd and the Aesir as most prominent Gods.

It has several problems mostly the several flirts of white-racist and neo-nazis. Actually during the Third Reich under the leading hand of Himmler there was a new reconstruction going on as the original religion of the Arian peoples. Today this problem still exist, owners – not moderators - of asatru forums often turn out to be racist. Also, a lot of literature and organizations either refer to or have (in)direct ties with racist writers/organizations. It should be noted that most Asatruar are clearly anti-racist and often engage in angry debates with racist, self-described 'asatruar'.

See   Asatruar

          Heathenry

          NeoPaganism

Asatruar

A practitioner of the religion of Asatru.

See   Asatrr

          Heathenry

          Heathen

ƀ

Benandanti

Literally meaning 'good walker'. The benandanti were Shamanic 'warriors' in a rural region of north Italy. They fought for the harvest against the malandanti or the 'Witches' at specific nights usually coinciding with 1 may, 1 february, 1 august, 1 november and around the winter and summer solstice. They went out at night, fighting in 'divisions' led by a captain who would beat them up if they told anyone, in a meadow they fought for the Faith of Christ against the evil Witches who fought for the Faith of the Devil. If they won the harvest would be prosperous and if they lost the harvest would be bad. The early Benandanti testimonies tell us about the Benandanti as Shamanic 'warriors' going out "in love of the grain". However, their myth became altered by the growing fear of Witches and in the end they convinced themselves that they were Witches, denoting their end. This was all beautifully recorded by Carlo Ginzburg.

See   Witch hunts

C

Calamus
Also known as sweet flag. When drunk as a tea the dried root can produce hallucinations. Sometimes used as an entheogen. Supposedly an ingredient of the legendary drink absinth.

See   Entheogen

Cosmology
The study and make up of the Cosmos – often portraying how the Universe is made up out of several worlds and what binds them together.

Crooked Path
The crooked path is a phrase used to denote the 'other path' – i.e. the Old Ways.

See   Traditional Witchcraft

Crooked Path
A podcast (internet radio programme) for "modern cunning folk"

and is the only podcast for Traditional Witches currently. It can be considered rather influential and has taken in it's wide course an almost encyclopaedically volume, at least 70 episodes with each episode containing information about the Old Ways and especially Traditional Witchcraft. Also contains interviews with controversial people, or people with controversial stories such as Robin Artisson and the leaders of the Roebuck about the death of Robert Cochrane.

d

Devil, the
The Devil is thought of by the Christians as the satanic majesty ruling the Underworld. Often he is conceived as a malign being trying to hurt ("innocent") Christians. It should be said that in popular folktales the Devil also functions as a comical figure. Though the Devil rose independently of the Heathen religion some of the aspects of the Pagan (male) Gods have been assumed into its figure, such as the goat's horns, the horse's hooves and more general symbolism. In one Dutch medieval story the Devil is depicted with one eye, just like Odin.

See   Witchcraft
        Diablo Stigmata

Diablo Stigmata
Latin name for the infamous Witches' Mark, which was given to the Witch by the Devil as a result of a bite or blood-letting at her initiation. The Witches Mark was conceived as the regular mole, scar or any other deformation of the human skin. Used as one of the ways to identify a Witch.

See   Devil, the
        Witchcraft

e

Edda, Poetic
A collection of Old Norse Poems collected in Norway and generally Scandinavia during the Christianized period. It tells several
stories in poetic form of the Gods, the origins and end of the
World, also several hero-tales.

See   Edda, Prose
         Mythology, Norse

Edda, Prose
Snorri Sturluson wrote this book, often referring to the Heathen
Gods, as a how-too book for Skalds, Old Norse poets. This book
is said to help you understand what it going on in the Poetic
Edda, as Snorri comments upon the Poetic Edda continuously.

See   Edda, Poetic
         Mythology, Norse

Entheogen
Form of, often herbal, substance which is used to as drug. Instead
of focussing on the recreational value the entheogen is applied as
strictly spiritual tool and often considered 'sacred' as the entheogen is often believed to open up the mind to the God.

f

Familiar
The Witches' Familiar was said to be a personal aid in the form of
an animal given to the Witch by the Devil during her initiation.
Often the familiar would be kept around the house and often fed
by 'power' drained from the Witches' Mark. The familiar would

often carry the Witch to the Sabbath. The familiar is often considered the physical manifestation of the Fetch/Fylgia.

See   Fetch
        Fylgia
        Witch hunts

Fetch
A name used by Traditional Witches to describe their soul. Also used to denote the animalistic side of the Witch's being. The Fetch has a lot in common with the fylgia only differing in the aspect of animal appearance. Though the fylgia can also some sort of 'Godmother' the Fetch only appears as an animal and sometimes as an elf-woman. Sending forth the Fetch refers to the practice of shape shifting and astral travel.

See   Fylgia
        Familiar

Fly Agaric
See Amanita Muscaria

Fylgia
Literally meaning 'double' or 'follower'. An animal conceived by the Old Norse as an animal living separately from the human mind in the human body. Can leave the body when the mind is asleep. Conceived as part of the essential soul. Without the fylgia a human could not exist and would die.

See   Fetch
        Familiar
        Mythology, Norse

g

Grimoire
A 'grammaire', or grammar' of magick, telling you how to make
magic. Famous grimoires such as the Key of Salomon the King
and The Threefold Coercion of Hell, depict ritual magic systems
depicting several procedures by which infernal spirits could be
tamed and summoned.

h

Heathen
Coming from the saying 'from the heath' meaning the person
was backwards i.e. non-Christian. Often the people living 'on the
heath' or outside the normal village and civilization retained a
more ancient, more Pagan way of life and still worshipped the old
Gods. Today the word is used to denote people following a form
of reconstructionist Heathenry, mostly Celtic or Germanic in
origin. The asatruar are one form of Heathen and often the term
is used interchangeably though actually it also refers to all Pagan
practices of northern Europe while asatruar refers only to people
loyal to the Aesir and not to the people loyal to the Vanir or just
'regular' Heathens who worship some local God or being. Also it
can be used to describe people who still walk the Old Ways, still
keep the Old View alive.

See   Heathenry
       Asatru
       Asatruar
       Paganism

Heathenry
A general term for the beliefs and religious practices of Pagans.
Used in asatru-circles as name for the Teutonic Paganism, en-

compassing both Germanic and Norse reconstructionist Pagans. Often Heathenry is based upon beliefs found in the Edda's but base themselves as well upon continental practices, depending upon geographical location.

See   Asatru
        Paganism
        Traditional Witchcraft
        HegdeWitchery

Hedge-Rider

A term denoting (Germanic) Shamans functioning as travellers between the Otherworlds. The term 'Hedgerider' means that the person upon the hedge finds him/herself upon the boundary between the worlds, and so has the ability to engage in contact with beings and forces of both worlds. Legacy of the Hedgerider continued during the persecution of the Witches, who can be seen as their legitimate heirs.

See   HedgeWitchy
        Traditional Witchcraft
Seiðr
        Seiðkona
        Shamanism
        Witchcraft
        Heathenry

HedgeWitch

Of course a name used for a practitioner of HedgeWitchy, used for Witches displaying the same characteristics as the 'Hedgerider'. Basically a later name for 'Hedgerider'.

See   HedgeWitchy
        Hedgerider
        Traditional Witchcraft

HedgeWitchery
Term first used by Rae Beth to denote a solitairy Wiccan Witch.
However, the name actually refers to a type of Witchery practiced
by the Hedgerider and can thus be considered essentially Shamanic. HedgeWitchery is the/a Germanic form of Shamanisn.

See   Hedgerider
        Traditional Witchcraft
        Heathenry
        Witchcraft
        Shamanism
        Seiðr
        Neo-Wicca

Hell
Realm of the dead in Teutonic Mythology. though Hell is conceived by Christians as a place of eternal punishment there is no
reason to assume it was the same to Heathens. They thought of
it as a place of both joy and punishment. The information we
have about the conception of Hell is heavily tainted by Christian
writer's impressions and deformations.

Herodias
A biblical figure attribute to be the Queen of the Witches by the
Inquisition. Originally this figure had no such connection.

Hexe
German name for the English 'Witch'. Is pronounced practically
the same as the Dutch heks and both stem from a root meaning
'Hedgerider'.

See   Witchcraft
        HedgeWitchy
        Hedgerider

Hex
'to hex' means 'to curse' or to charm someone. In this book however it is used as the name of the continental Witches. For a full explanation see Hexe.

See   Witchcraft
Witch
HedgeWitchy

Holda
Coming from a root meaning 'hollow'. Continuation of the Great Goddes of the Indo-Europeans. Her lore is more intact on the continent and her rites continued well into medieval and sometimes even renaissance times. Her aspect are threefold, i.) Goddes of Fate ii.) Goddess of the Underworld iii.) Goddess of the Earth and Abundance. These three aspects picture her as a Goddess with a dark and bright side. For a more full description see chapter three.

Holle
A name for the Witch-Goddess native to Holland and western /south-western Germany. For a full explanation see Holda

Hulda
A Danish name for the Witch-Goddess. For a full explanation see Holda.

m

Mark, Witches'
See Diablo Stigmata

Middle-Earth
The dimension Earth, suited at the middle of the World-Tree and can be seen as the 'middle layer' of the threefold unity, Underworld, Middle Earth and Heavens.

Midgard
Old Norse name for Middle-Earth, see Middle Earth

See   Mythology, Norse

Mugwort
See Artimesia Vulgaris

Mythos
A full, working body of mythology. often used as name of a collectively accepted body of lore specific to a certain tradition, religion or group. Also the name of a greek beer.

See   Mythology
        Mythology, Norse

Mythology
A set of beliefs blindly accepted which give a explanation of the world. Mythology should not be taken literally and can be seen as a metaphysical conception of the world rather than a direct explanation of its origins.

See   Mythology, Norse

Mythology, Norse
Mythology of the Old Norse peoples collected during the period 10th-13th century, mostly in Iceland as this wasn't violently Christianized.

See   Heathenry
        Edda, Poetic

Edda, Prose
Asatruar
Seiðr

n

NeoPagan

Name for reconstructionist Pagan, meaning he or she has no
experience of living in a Heathen culture. Also a name spit at by
Heathens and Traditional Witches and is almost exclusively used
by new-age Wiccans though realistically applies to practically
every modern Pagan movement.

See   Traditional Witchcraft
        Heathenry
        Neo-Wicca
        Asatru
        HegdWitchery

Neo-Wicca

Name used for New-Age branch of Wicca, which is 'Wiccan-
esque' in nature meaning it doesn't fit into the British Traditional
Wiccan structure but does call itself Wiccan or has obvious Wiccan leanings. Neo-Wicca is eclectical in nature and takes parts
form several traditions either forming a new traditions or just taking and discarding parts until eternity. Often considered 'fluffy'
and 'simple-minded'.

See   NeoPagan
        Wiccan

Nidhög

Serpent-dragon being in Norse Mythology and is said to tear the
sinful dead apart at the Corpse Shore.

See   Norse Mythology

Niflheim
Name means 'mist-world' and was one of the two opposites of frost-fire from which Ginnungagap was created. Also name for the Underworld in Norse Mythology. thought of as a bigger realm with Hell lying in it. Also the realm where the Seething cauldron, the Well of Wyrd and the well of wisdom are suited.

See   Norse Mythology
        Hell

Norse Mythology

See   mythology, Norse

O

Odin
Name for the Allfather of the Norse Pantheon. Functions as the God of (poetic) Inspiration, death, the dead, wisdom, War and some say the Underworld. He is considered the chief God of the Aesir and was one of the most important Gods.

See   Old Gods

Old Gods
Name used in Traditional Witchcraft and occasionally in Heathenry to signify the Heathen Deities, or the Deities of the Witches. "Old" refers to the idea of the 'true', 'first' Gods, being kicked out by the Christians.

See   Holda
        Odin

Old Ways
Name denoting the ancestral (Heathen) beliefs of our forebears.

The old ways range from the Cunning Folk traditions to the reconstructionist practices of the Asatruar.

See   HedgeWitchy
        Traditional Witchcraft
        Asatru
        Heathenry

ᛈ

Pagan
A believer of Paganism.

See   Paganism

Paganism
A form of spiritual belief, nature-based often, which isn't conform to the monotheistic, Judeo-Christian idea of 'good' spirituality. Paganism is a term used to refer to the nature religions of all around the world.

See   NeoPaganism
        Heathenry

Passionflower
See Passiflora Incarnata

Passiflora Incarnata
Plant which is sometimes used as an entheogen. also has beautiful flower. For a fuller description see Chapter Five.

See   entheogen

Perchta
Name for the Witch-Goddess and a manifestation of Holda.

See   Holda

Poetic Edda
See   Edda, Poetic

Prose Edda
See   Edda, Prose

R

Robert Cochrane
Traditional Witch who opposed the Gardnerian movement in the 1960's. Magister, that means leader, of the Clan of Tubal Cain in which he taught his form of Traditional Witchcraft. The first Traditional Witch to write openly about his beliefs. Unfortunately he died as a result of suicide. His legacy continues in his writings and letters which are found in 'the writings and letter of Robert Cochrane' and "The Roebuck in the Thicked".

See   Traditional Witchcraft
        1734-tradition
        1734

S

Sabbati Uguenti
Latin name for the notorious flying ointment. Flying ointments were prepared out of certain alkaloid-containing herbs which were then rubbed onto the skin of the Witch, chemically invoking sensations of flying and all sorts of pleasures. Can be considered

an entheogen, even though the recipes have been lost.

See   Entheogen

Seiðr

Old Norse Shamanic practice in which the practitioner would sit on a platform and engage in a trance by which the practitioner could leave the body, see into the other worlds and predict the future. A practice very akin to Witchery, they seem to have originated from the same source. Practitioners of Seiðr weren't as highly valued as the Volva and were occasionally lynched by angry mobs.

See   Seiðkona
         Seidmadr
         Shamanism
         Heathenry
         Mythology, Norse
         Hedge-Rider
         HedgeWitchy

Seiðkona

Female practitioner of Seiðr.

See   Seidr
         Hedgerider
         HedgeWitchy
         Shamanism

Seiðmaðr

Male practitioner of Seiðr, Seiðr was considered a dishonourable practice for men as it had connotations of sex-changing, thought to be unsuitable for a man of honour.

See   Seidr
         Seidkona

Hedgerider
Shamanism
Odin

Shaman
Practitioner of Shamanism.

See   Shamanism

Shamanism
Set of practices and beliefs in which the Shaman engages in contact with the Under- and Upperworlds.

See   Shaman

Sisters, Wyrd
See   Wyrd sisters

Stang
Comes from the Old Norse word meaning 'pole'. A forked branch of wood historically used by Witches to travel to the Sabbath/the Underworld. Also used in the rites of Traditional Witches and the rites of Freyr.

U

Underworld
Word referring to the underground realm inhabited by dark and mysterious forces. Also the dead are said to dwell here. The Underworld in Teutonic Mythology is guarded by a Dog and is separated from the world of the living by a huge, ice-cold river. The Underworld is also the realm in which the Well is positioned, thought of in Norse mythology as threefold (and Is depicted

separate), the Well of Wyrd, the well of wisdom and the Seething cauldron/well of waters/Rivers. According to this book the Underworld was the centre of a Shamanic Cult of Witches/ Hedgerider who engaged in contact with, arousal of, and journeys to the Underworld.

See   Hedgerider
        Hell
        HedgeWitchy
        Heathenry
        Asatru
        Traditional Witchcraft
        Seidr

V

Vallhöl
Realm in the heavens in which dead warriors, chosen by Odin, live. Here they feast and fight until the Doom of the Gods. Only the warriors who died bravely and in battle were admitted into this realm, also people, they thought, who had dedicated their lives to Odin could be admitted into these realm.

See   Odin
        Mythology, Norse

Venusberg
Mountain in Germany, often attributed to the Horselberg, in which a legendary Elf-Queen lived, often called Frau Holle. In this mountain Shamanic travellers reported, often erotic, games and revelry.

See   Holda
        Witches

Witchcraft
HedgeWitchy
Hedgerider

Völva
Priestess in Old Norse society. They functioned as intermediary between the Gods and the humans. Also they possessed spectacular oracular and magical skills, by which they could predict the future – sometimes even outwitting the Gods in their skill and knowledge. Some of the Völva were practitioners of Seiðr. Probably their practices were very akin and could hardly be distinguished by the outsider. Point is, Seiðkona was seen as 'malign' while the Völva was respected and even played their role in the dealings of the kings – portraying the Völva as a deeply respectable woman.

See   Seiðr
       Seiðkona
       Seiðmaðr
       Hedgerider
       Heathenry
       Shamanism

ᛈ

Weird Sisters
Name from Shakespeares Macbeth used for the three Witches who predict the king's death. Late name for the Wyrd Sisters, see Wyrd Sisters.

See   Wyrd

Wicca – British Traditional
Wiccan traditions stemming from either a Gardnerian (from the late Gerald B. Gardner) or Alexandrian (from Alex Sanders, a

more ceremonial variation upon the Gardnerian tradition). These two traditions, or crossings such as Al-Gard traditions, can be seen as the only two 'legitimite', meaning definable, traditions of Wicca. Their main characteristic is the use of the Three Degree initiation and a copy of the original Gardnerian/Alexandrian Book of Shadows. Though every individual group is allowed some space of filling in certain facets of the tradition, they work along a coherent framework and system which is continuous since the conception of Wicca in the fifties and sixties of the 20th century. Most of the British Traditional Wiccans acknowledge the fact that their beliefs and practices were formed from elements of Qaballa, Ritual Magick, Ceremonial Magick, especially Golden Dawn esoteric elements, and the theories of Dr. Margaret Murray, though still keeping to the point that their beliefs are relevant and meaningful.

See   Neo-Wicca
       Witchcraft
       Wiccan

Wicca – Non-British Traditional
See   Neo-Wicca

Wiccan
Follower of the religion/life-style of Wicca, either a British Traditionalist or Eclectic.

See   Neo-Wicca
       Witchcraft
       NeoPagan

Witch
Practitioner of Witchcraft. Can be either male or female though historically was only apllied to women; though men were also practitioners of Witchcraft these were often given the name

'Witchmaster' or 'warlock'. Today people calling themselves Witches are either (eclectic) Wiccan, Traditional/Hereditairy, female (LaVeyan) Satanist, or own to a specific cultural tradition/frame work. Most of the time the different groups deny each other the right to call one self "Witch".

See   Witchcraft
        Hexe
        Hegderider
        HedgeWitchery
        Traditional Witchcraft
        Wicca – British Traditional
        Neo-Wicca

Witchcraft

Witchcraft is differently defined by different groups and movements and so there is no one, collectively approved definition. There are several forms of Witches and the different forms of "Witchcraft" are given under the movement's specific name.

See   Witch
        HedgeWitchery
        Neo-Wicca
        Wicca – British Traditional

Witch-hunts

Phenomena in which, often imaginary, 'Witches' were prosecuted. This took place already in the second half of the middle ages (after 1000) and evolved into the, religiously and politically motivated and propagated, and, it should be mentioned opposed, Witchcraze. In this period, which was at it worst during the 16th century, it sometimes took the form of mass murder – once accused the "Witch" had no opportunity of a proper, just procedure and there was no possibility of escaping from the fire. During the medieval period the prosecution of Witches was less harsh often resulting in exile and fines rather than death sentences.

See   Witch
         Witchcraft
         Witches' Mark
         Devil, the

Witches' Mark
See Diablo Stigmata

Wodan
Germanic version of Odin.

See   Odin

Wyrd
Name referring to the concept 'Fate'. In this it is believed that Fate is inevitable and by the condition from early childhood one can't escape this choice and so one is doomed to follow a certain way. Though Fate admits the possibility of endless opportunities it denies Free Will as one is Fated to make a certain choice, as ones personality is defined by earlier conditions and experiences.

See   Wyrd Sisters
         Holda
         Heathenry

Wyrd Sister
Three "sisters' of Wyrd, Fate. They appear in Norse mythology under different names and appear also throughout folkore of the continent. Correspond to the Greek Fates. The Wyrd sisters are the Goddesses of Fate of which one spins the thread of Fate, the other weaves it into existence and the other cuts it.

See   Wyrd
         Heathenry
         Holda

Appendix: Book Hoard

Works of Historical, Mythological, Folkloric and Botanical Reference

Carlo Ginzburg, Ecstasies: deciphering the Witches' Sabbath
1990, Hutchinson Radius
0 09 174024

Hilda Roderick Ellis, The Road to Hell: A study of the Conception of the dead in Old Norse Literature
1943, Cambridge University Press
No ISBN mentioned

Carlo Ginzburg, Extasen: een oncijfering van de heksenSabbath
1993, Uitgeverij Wereldbibliotheek
90 284 1672

Carlo Ginzburg, De Benandanti: hekserij en vruchtbaarheidsriten in de 16e en 17e eeuw
1986, Bert Bakker
90 351 0300 9

 Hans Peter Duerr, Dreamtime: Concerning the Boundary between Wilderness and Civilization
1985, Basil Blackwell
0 631 13375

Richard Cavendish, The Black Arts: A concise history of Witchcraft, demonology, astrology, alchemy and other mystical practices throughout the ages
1968, Penguin Books
9780399500350

M. Grieve, A Modern Herbal Vol I
1971, Dover Publications
0 486 22789 7

M. Grieve, A Modern Herbal Vol II
1971, Dover Publications
0 486 22789 5

Kurt BaschWitch, Heksen en heksenprocessen
1964, Synopsis
90 295 0121 9

Jan de Zutter, Eko Eko: een halve eeuw Wicca
2003, houtekiet
905240 733

Gebroeders Grimm, Sprookjes voor kind en gezin
1974, Lemniscaat
90 6069 168 7

Anna Franklin & Paul Mason, Fairy Lore
1999, Capall Bann Publishing
1861607 3

 Grimm, Teutonic Mythology
1828, http://www.northvegr.org/lore/grimmst/

Viktor Rydberg, Teutonic Mythology
1907, http://www.vaidilute.com/books/norroena/rydberg-con-
tents.html

Alby Stone, The Knots of death
Web of Wyrd nr. 7, http://www.sacred-texts.com/bos/bos649.htm

Laurentius, Knappert, De Beteekenis van de wetenschap van het folklore voor de Godsdienst geschiedenis onderzocht en aan den holda mythen getoetst
1887, http://www.nissaba.nl/holda/index.htm

Max Dashu, The Tregenda of the Old Goddess, Witches and Spirits
2000, http://www.suppressedhistories.net/secrethistory/Witchtregenda.html

Alby Stone, Hellhound, werewolves and the Germanic Underworld
1994, http://www.indigogroup.co.uk/edge/Hellhnds.htm

Not Mentioned, Holda and the Cult of the Witches
Not Mentioned, http://www.ealdriht.org/Witchholda.html

Henry Adam Bellows, Poetic Edda
1936 , http://www.cybersamurai.net/Mythology/NorseMyth.htm

John D. Seymour, Irish Witchcraft & Demonology: CHPT. II
Dame Alice Kyteler, the sorceress of Kilkenny
1913, http://www.sacred-texts.com/pag/iwd/iwd03.htm

Unknown, Online Etymoligical Dictionairy
Retrieved Okt. 2007, http://www.etymonline.com/

Works of Intellectual, Philosophical, Spiritual and Ritual Reference

Yngona Desmond, Völuspá – seiðr as Wyrd consciousness
2005, no company mentioned
14196 1841 5

Jan Fries, Seidways: shaking, swaying and serpent mysteries
1996, Mandrake of Oxford

1 869928 36 9

Evan John Jones & Robert Cochrane, The Roebuck in the Thicket: An Anthology of the Robert Cochrane Witchcraft Tradition
2001, Capall Bann Publishing
186163 1553

Gwyn, Light from the Shadows: a Mythos of Modern Traditional Witchcraft
1999, Capall Bann Publishing
186163 0638

Robin Artisson, The Witching Way of the hollow hill
2005, Owlblink Bookcrafting Company
No ISBN mentioned

Kenneth Johnson, North Star Road: Shamanism, Witchcraft and the Otherworld journey
1996, Llewellyn Publications
1 56718 370 0

R.J. Stewart, Collected Articles
Unknown, http://www.dreampower.com/articles.html

Robert Cochrane, The Writings & Letters of Robert Cochrane
1960's , http://www.cyberWitch.com/bowers/akc.htm

Peter Paddon, The Crooked Path: a podcast for modern cunning folk
2006-7, http://www.crookedpath.org/show.html

Index

Libro de Varie Storie, 31
Livonia, 98, 105
Loki, 114
Lord of Dread, 136, 138
Love, 53, 105, 128-129, 154
M. Grieve, 176
M. R. Ellis, 65
Madame Oriente, 13, 16, 31-32
Magister, 166
Magus, 95
Male, 15, 49, 51, 130, 155, 167, 171
Malkuth, 74
Maria, 48, 139
Maria Light Mass, 139
Mariënfaden, 48
Mark, 82, 104, 108, 122-123, 155-156, 161, 173
Master, 68-69, 74, 98, 124, 138
Matron of Marriage, 53
Max Dashu, 177
May Eve, 50
Meadow, 16, 92, 98, 105, 108, 154
Meal, 67
Mecklenburg, 48
Medieval, 13, 20, 30, 48, 50, 53, 84, 99, 104, 119, 134, 141, 155, 161, 172
Menglo, 128
Mention, 22, 135
Mentioned, 15, 56-57, 72, 107, 130, 151, 172, 175, 177-178

Mephistopheles, 119
Meschino, 31
Metaphysics of Hell, 5, 25
Mid-World, 33
Middle Dutch, 11
Middle Earth, 39, 55, 162
Midgard, 26, 37, 47, 72, 162
Midwinter, 29, 47
Mimameid, 72
Mimir, 5, 34, 65, 72, 75
Mimirs Well, 35
Mind, 12, 19, 33, 36, 38, 43, 62, 75-76, 78, 81, 86, 89-93, 107, 118, 122, 128, 131-132, 152, 156-157
Mind-based, 5, 76-77, 90
Mind-Based Techniques, 5, 76-77, 90
Misrule, 47, 67
Modern Paganism, 5, 17
Modern Wiccans, 10
Modern Witches, 17
Mother, 10, 22, 33, 43, 45, 47-48, 52, 54-56, 84, 121, 128, 138
Mother Goose, 84
Mother Nature, 43
Mountain, 30-31, 33, 47, 49-50, 57, 92-93, 119, 169
Mugwort, 5, 78, 83-89, 109, 124, 152, 162
Musings, 7, 133
Muslim, 43
Muspelheim, 26
Mysteries, 64, 96, 177
Mystery, 12-13, 35, 38, 62,

191

Breinigsville, PA USA
08 December 2010
250909BV00003B/77/P